"In this book, [the authors] go beyond the usual ways we think about anger, and bring new depth to the subject. [They are] masters at providing astute and warmhearted guidance for working with this difficult emotion."

—Sasha Loring, MEd, LCSW, author of *RELIEF: Release Stress and Harmful Habits and Awaken Your Best Self* and *Eating with Fierce Kindness*

"Using personal portrayals and easy, practical exercises anyone can do anytime, this encouraging handbook teaches us how we can mindfully transform the destructive flames of anger into the alchemical fires of profound healing and liberating joy! A true gem and 'must-read' for those who wrestle with anger, for the professionals who offer support, and for all of us as we experience the very real and profoundly human emotion of anger."

—Maya McNeilly, PhD, licensed clinical and health psychologist, and MBSR instructor at Duke Integrative Medicine

"Jeffrey Brantley and Wendy Millstine offer their readers a treasure trove of resources for understanding and befriending the difficult emotion of anger. Infused with the wisdom of their own life practice, the book is filled with meditations that help cultivate mindfulness, cool the fires of anger, open the heart with compassion, and transform one's relationship to life."

—Phyllis Hicks, psychotherapist, meditation student, and teacher

"[The authors'] profound respect and compassion for people, in our beauty and our pain, shine through these writings. The practices are skillfully presented. They are simple, doable, and deeply effective."

—**Kim Warren, MA, MS**, meditator, small business owner, and caregiver

"This clear and accessible guide reflects the decades of personal and professional experience of a key leader in the field of mindfulness as he offers simple and skillful ways to work with anger. Mindfulness professionals will appreciate his fresh perspective on classic mindfulness teachings. All looking for another way to work with forms of anger, ranging from the simmering of irritation to the large flames of rage, will learn how to transform these fiery energies without being burned. The specific, practical examples offered instill the reader with courage and confidence to experiment with new approaches to this challenging mind state."

—**Julie Kosey, MS, PCC, RYT**, professional certified coach, mindfulness and yoga teacher, and founder and owner of Mindful Moments, LLC

"If you yearn for understanding of your anger, this book is like a clearing in the middle of a chaos, arising from much experience, deep kindness, and care in skillful presentation. It guides you in disengaging from anger, shows you how to cool down these sensations, and teaches you to transform any strong emotions over time. In the process, you find a way to your inherent goodness, learn to embrace impermanence, and transcend the commonly held ideas of healing and peace."

—Riitta H. Rutanen Whaley, MS, MSPH,
founder of Yoga for Life, LLC; certified yoga
teacher (RYT); and MBSR instructor at
Duke Integrative Medicine

"In their latest companion book, Jeffrey Brantley and Wendy Millstine share their personal experiences and insights about how to gain greater clarity and control over anger through mindfulness. Well organized, clear, authentic, and practical, I highly recommend this book as a skillful means to learning how to approach anger without fear, but rather with kindness, curiosity, and compassion."

—Jeffrey M. Greeson, PhD, MS, assistant
professor of clinical psychology in psychiatry,
University of Pennsylvania, Perelman School
of Medicine

"It has been said that dealing with anger can be like holding on to a hot coal. We may be right, but it is us suffering the damage. In this book, [the authors share] skills of mindfulness and practical wisdom that [they have] developed from years of meditation practice and helping people with difficult life experiences. Here are real ways to let go of anger and become more free."

> —Jon Seskevich, RN, BSN, CHTP, award-winning nurse clinician, pioneer in holistic nursing and integrative healing, and adjunct faculty member at the University of North Carolina, School of Nursing

"The authors provide a welcome addition to the emerging applications of mindfulness by offering a practical blueprint for transforming the challenging emotion of anger into greater wisdom, mercy, and well-being. Practices designed to enhance attention, compassion, and insight gently guide the reader through the 'doorway of anger' toward a deeper understanding of its causes and conditions. This book brings to light the power of mindfulness to move one beyond the constrictions of anger and toward greater freedom and interconnection with all of life as it is being lived, moment by moment."

> —Ron Vereen, MD, psychiatrist in private practice, Durham, NC; consulting associate in the department of psychiatry and behavioral sciences at Duke University; MBSR instructor at Duke Integrative Medicine; and cofounder of the Triangle Insight Meditation Community

daily meditations for calming your angry mind

mindfulness practices to free yourself from anger

JEFFREY BRANTLEY, MD
WENDY MILLSTINE, NC

New Harbinger Publications, Inc.

Publisher's Note

Distributed in Canada by Raincoast Books

Copyright © 2015 by Jeffrey Brantley and Wendy Millstine
New Harbinger Publications, Inc.
5674 Shattuck Avenue
Oakland, CA 94609
www.newharbinger.com

Cover design by Amy Shoup; Text design by Amy Shoup and Michele Waters-Kermes; Acquired by Tesilya Hanauer; Edited by Jean Blomquist

Library of Congress Cataloging-in-Publication Data

Brantley, Jeffrey.
  Daily meditations for calming your angry mind : mindfulness practices to free yourself from anger / Jeffrey Brantley, Wendy Millstine.
    pages cm
  Includes bibliographical references.
  ISBN 978-1-62625-167-0 (paperback) -- ISBN 978-1-62625-168-7 (pdf-ebook) -- ISBN 978-1-62625-169-4 (epub) 1. Anger. 2. Meditation. I. Millstine, Wendy, 1966- II. Title.
  BF575.A5.B7384 2015
  152.4'7--dc23
                                  2015010159

17   16   15

10 9 8 7 6 5 4 3 2 1   First printing

This book is dedicated to my dear wife, Mary, whose love and compassion have blessed and transformed my life.

—Jeffrey Brantley

This book is dedicated to all those who struggle with anger. May these practices help you find deep compassion and loving acceptance for yourself, and may you find balance, equanimity and emotional healing along the way. I am also dedicating this book to my dad, Albert Jack Millstine (1928–2005), who taught me the ability to understand and accept painful emotions, the courage to learn from my own anger, and the wisdom and rewards of forgiveness. He will always be remembered as a mighty warrior for love in my heart.

—Wendy Millstine

Contents

PART 2
MEDITATIONS FOR CALMING YOUR ANGRY MIND AND LIVING WITH GREATER JOY AND EASE

CHAPTER 5
Calming Your Angry Mind at Work   135

CHAPTER 6
Beyond Your Angry Mind: Practices for Living with More Joy and Peace in Every Moment 167

Preface

There is an old story about a couple caught offshore in a small rowboat when a storm comes up. The one rowing the boat stops, drops her oars, and brings her hands together in a prayer position. The wind howls, rain falls in buckets, and the waves grow larger by the minute. The other person yells, "What are you doing?" The rower answers, "I am praying for our safety." The other person yells back, "Pray to God, but row to shore!"

Do you ever feel like the people in that rowboat? Have intense bursts of anger, irritation, or disdain or feelings of impatience, criticism, or rejection too often become storms that threaten your life? Have you ever felt helpless before waves of negative emotions or, at times perhaps, felt that only divine intervention could save you from the painful feelings related to anger and ill will in your life? Do you endure portions of each day tense and on guard? Have the storms of anger caused you to lose touch with feelings of wonder, hope, joy, and the preciousness of life—the preciousness of your *own* life?

If you answered yes to any or all of those questions, the good news is you are not alone. And the really good news is that you *can* learn to enjoy yourself more, get unstuck from anger faster, and become more resilient and responsive to the challenges, obstacles, and stressors you experience in life. You do not have to lose hope about life or about yourself. You can find a peaceful, enduring center at the heart of any struggle or storm. Right now you may be thinking, *How? How can I find that peaceful center?* That's what this book is about.

The way to that peaceful, enduring center is through *mindfulness.* Mindfulness is awareness—a nonjudging awareness that is centered in the present moment. Mindfulness is about paying attention, without judgment, to the flow of your thoughts, feelings, and physical sensations in each and every moment. Mindfulness is always available to you and will help you tap deeply into positive inner resources, qualities, and capacities that you already possess. Mindfulness enables you, in each moment and with each breath, to access that peaceful, enduring center—*even* when you feel angry. Not only can mindfulness help to calm your angry mind, it can also help you live your life with more joy and ease.

This book will be your guide to finding that peaceful, enduring center through mindfulness. We'll introduce you to the practice of mindfulness meditation and show how you can incorporate it into your daily life so you can tap your inner resources, understand your anger better, and free yourself from its toxic impact. But before we do that, we want to introduce ourselves. Because mindfulness has played and continues to play such an important role in our own lives, we want to share its benefits with others, including you. That's why we've written this book, and we want you do know how mindfulness has helped us in our lives.

JEFF'S STORY

As a young man growing up in North Carolina, I noticed anger in the adults and children around me, and at times I felt hurt from that anger. Of course, I became angry too. I am sure that my own expressions of anger over the years caused hurt in others, and I am now very sorry, looking back, for any hurt to others my anger may have caused. Despite these expressions of anger around and by me, though, I don't recall many conversations about anger, and somehow, I think, I got the impression that it was not a good thing to be angry.

As I grew older, making my way through high school and college, I never thought much about what being angry meant. However, I do recall, somewhere along the way, having a vague idea that when a "man" (whatever that meant) got really angry, he had to take some kind of action, possibly violent, but somehow justified. Where that idea came from, I can only guess.

I also know that I still hadn't really thought much about my own anger (or paid much attention to the feeling of anger in my heart, mind, and body) until I entered psychotherapy during my years as a psychiatry resident at UC Irvine in Southern California. For about two of those years, I was a patient in a Gestalt therapy group. For a time during those two years, I was going through a painful period in my personal life and experienced a lot of confused feelings, including angry ones.

In one of those therapy sessions, when I mentioned feeling angry, the male coleader invited me to "get it out" using a kind of plastic bat called a *bataka*. This meant that we each picked up a bataka and started hitting at each other, but striking only at the bats themselves, not at the other person. As the session went on, we really went at it, and I still recall burning with anger as I swung that bataka. Then the therapist said he had to stop because he had hurt his hand. I found out later that one of my strikes had actually broken a bone in his hand where he held his bataka! He and I laughed about it, and there were no hard feelings, but I know I thought more about different ways of "getting in touch" with anger and getting anger "out" after that!

Interestingly enough, some years later on a meditation retreat with the Buddhist monk Thich Nhat Hanh, I recalled this experience and resonated deeply with Nhat Hanh's observation that we can unintentionally create more anger and its harmful effects if we are not mindful. He pointed out that when we are not mindful, we often don't realize how we make our own anger stronger or perhaps even create new anger as we are acting it out.

Over the years, I have learned more about myself and about anger as I have practiced psychiatry and psychotherapy, studied and practiced mindfulness and meditation, and have worked with others in these realms. One of the most important things I have come to understand is that my personal experience with anger is not uncommon. Like me—especially before I came to psychotherapy and mindfulness—many people have little or no awareness of anger in themselves, but they feel hurt from the anger in others. They also form mistaken or incomplete ideas about anger (and other emotions), don't know what to do about their anger, and suffer because of it.

I hope that this book, and the efforts that I, Wendy, and the people at New Harbinger have made creating it, will help, at least in some small way, to ease the pain of anger and intolerance in our world. Where there is anger, I hope this book will help you and others find wisdom, mercy, and well-being. And when there is difficulty, I hope this book and these practices will help you and others find, and respond from, the peaceful, enduring center at the heart of any struggle.

WENDY'S STORY

My interest in anger is very personal. As a child, I grew up in a home brimming with unconditional love and kindness from both of my parents—for the most part. I also shared a home with a dad who fought a battle with his inner demons under a storm of intense anger. Because I was a daddy's girl—and yearned for his constant attention, acceptance, and affection for as long as I can remember—I was forced to cautiously tiptoe in the shadow of an unpredictable rage that could be unleashed at any given moment over any given grievance, great or small. It didn't take much to set my dad's anger off—a misplaced tool in the garage, the car not starting, or the wrong response to something he said or asked for. Once he was mad, he reacted swiftly with a hailstorm of harsh words and actions. He didn't know any other way to respond to his pain and suffering. His father had responded the same way, I've been told.

Some years later, after I no longer lived at home, I came to a deeper understanding and place of forgiveness for my dad. I learned that my dad was a complex man who struggled every day of his life with chronic physical pain, depression, and feelings of unworthiness and failure. I was a young adult then, and with evolving maturity, I was able to embody more tenderness and compassion for my dad's limitations and lack of resources to adequately cope with his anger.

This is why the topic of this book and these techniques are crucial for me personally. I feel that it's imperative that I share what I've learned about anger. Anger affects everyone, and we all need more tools and resources to manage our anger. Mindfulness was first introduced to me about nine years ago, while I was studying holistic nutrition and the effects of meditation on diet and stress reduction. I learned firsthand the profoundly positive and healing effects that mindfulness meditation had both on others and on me for significantly improving health and overall well-being. I've been hooked on meditation ever since!

Mindfulness, as we mentioned above, is about paying attention to the precise moment-by-moment flow of your thoughts, feelings, and physical sensations without judgment. I discovered how the power of being in the unique unfolding of right here and now—following each inhale and exhale— radically transformed my relationship to painful and stressful situations. With practice, over time, mindfulness opened a door to experiencing these intense emotions and thoughts in a whole new way. In fact, I have come to learn that by mindfully turning toward and tuning in to my discomfort, I feel my discomfort loosen and dissipate. A daily informal mindfulness meditation also has taught me how to draw more easily from a bottomless well of profound empathy and compassion for others and myself. My mindfulness meditation has been a truly healing journey for me. I hope that you find the same healing as well.

I only wish that my dad were alive today so I could share this book with him. I know with certainty that he'd be proud of my efforts to help others. This book is a compassionate offering of deep-seated love and a strongly held belief in my dad, whose angry heart was never as big as his loving heart.

YOUR STORY: A NEW CHAPTER

Now we invite you to write a new chapter in your own life story as you encounter the transforming power of mindfulness. May the skills and practices we offer in the following chapters guide you to that peaceful, enduring center where your angry mind becomes calm and your life is filled with joy and ease.

PART I

Discovering the Power of Mindfulness

CHAPTER 1

Approaching Your
Anger Mindfully

You can be mindful of any human experience. *Being mindful* means stopping, noticing, and being aware of what is happening in the present moment without judging it. Being mindful also includes looking closely and being aware of what is happening in your inner life—the constantly changing thoughts, feelings, moods, and bodily sensations. Being mindful does not mean generating more thoughts, opinions, or feelings about what is here, or trying to change or fix anything. It is simply about stopping and watching with curiosity, kindness, and patience.

It has been said that being mindful is simplicity itself because you are not doing anything! You have stopped the "doing" (to or for anything) and are simply "being"—that is, being present and watchful. Stopping and being present is remarkably powerful. For example, when you stop to observe without judgments, and you are fully present, aware, and accepting, the things worrying you, the things you blame yourself for or things you feel despairing and vulnerable about, can come back into perspective. Being mindful, you immediately find yourself *here*— brightly and warmly alive—in the present moment. Stopping and seeing mindfully, with full acceptance of the present moment, makes the going forward in every dimension of your life richer, more palpable, and more heart-felt. For instance, pausing to be where you are (instead of in some imagined past or future) for a few mindful breaths before you enter your home after a busy work day can help you be fully present with focused and grateful attention, really feeling and responding to the embrace of your loved ones and completely hearing their words of greeting.

Being mindful is not passive, however. It takes effort, and, as we will see throughout this book, you will have to work at becoming more mindful if you wish to take back control of your life from anger and similar strong emotions.

Like other human beings, you are born with the capacity to be mindful. You already have all the mindfulness you need, at least potentially. Most people, though, have to learn how to tap that potential through practicing mindfulness and meditation if they wish to dwell more steadily in the peaceful, enduring center and to enjoy the amazing benefits that mindfulness offers. You can be mindful as part of a formal meditation practice where, for example, you might sit quietly and focus on your breathing. Or you can be mindful in a more informal way in any moment of daily living, if you stop and notice without judging—even for a single mindful breath or one mindful step.

You can, however, also be *mindless* during any human experience. You probably know the expression "going on automatic pilot," which captures the state of being mindless. It is a state of not noticing, of being unaware when something is happening. Mindlessness can occur, for example, when your attention is restless: your focus rapidly shifts from one thing to another and you miss something happening right in front of you. A familiar example of such mindlessness occurs when a friend speaks to you, but you don't hear the gist of what your friend says because your attention has already jumped someplace else.

You can be mindful or mindless of anger and other strong emotions, just as you can be mindful or mindless about any other human experience. You actually do have a choice to be mindful or mindless. And if you choose to be mindful, you can free yourself from the constricting impact of painful emotions.

Anger arises very quickly and often very painfully. Yet any time you are visited by anger, you can approach it mindfully. Learning to do this can take some work, but being mindful when you experience anger will enable you to acknowledge your anger without being controlled by it. Though you may find this hard to believe, it really is possible and definitely something that you can do!

On the other hand, if you are mindless about anger in your life—that is, if your anger is repeatedly unnoticed, chronically unmanaged, or poorly understood—you may experience angry thoughts and feelings frequently, and ultimately that anger can be harmful to your health. But your anger does not affect only you. When anger drives you to speak or act harshly toward others, your anger adds to the suffering and pain they may already feel. And even beyond those closest to you, when caught in the storm of anger, you add—even if unintentionally—to the general level of distress present in our world.

Yet, if you can stay present in that moment when anger burns within you and if you look closely enough, you can also find—right there in the very pain of anger—the possibility of radical and potent learning that can lead you to healing transformation. But how can healing begin with being angry? In any moment of anger, you might say that a door appears before you. It is a door created by your suffering. So, how can you open that door and move beyond your suffering? You open that door when you do three things: (1) you acknowledge that you are suffering, (2) you decide that you are tired of the suffering caused by your anger, and (3) you make a personal commitment to bring mindfulness into this moment of anger.

We want to help you open that door and to calm your angry mind by being mindful. This book is filled with mindfulness-based practices and exercises to help you grow mindful in your life. You will also discover how the power of mindfulness can help you understand, manage, and go beyond strong feelings like anger, ill will, and rejection, and end their power to cause pain and suffering for you and others. By working with these meditations, you can see for yourself what approaching anger mindfully can mean. You can find out for yourself that freedom from anger is an experience *you* can have in this life—it is not just a fantasy or somebody's theory, good for someone else perhaps, but not for you. This freedom *can* be yours.

In this chapter, you will learn more about mindfulness, the nature of anger, and three powerful paths for approaching anger mindfully. This knowledge will provide you with a foundation to support you as you explore and experiment with the mindfulness-based practices throughout this book. Now let's take a closer look at mindfulness.

MORE ABOUT MINDFULNESS

Mindfulness is a basic human quality and is the capacity for nonjudging awareness centered in the present moment. Mindfulness is also a way our minds function. Mindfulness is the "knowing" function of our minds, a function that is always there. But, although it's always there and always noticing everything going on around us, we don't always *recognize* this knowing and noticing because our minds move so quickly from knowing to doing. For example, let's say you notice (or "know") a beautiful sunset that moves you deeply. What happens then? Your mind begins scheduling you to come back every day at sundown to see more beautiful sunsets, and as you busily make plans to come to see future sunsets, you are no longer present for *this* sunset in *this* moment! To truly "know" or notice the sunset, you must allow your experience of the sunset to become a mindful moment.

So what exactly is a mindful moment? A *mindful moment* is a moment of being fully present and aware, and not distracted by all the judgments, commentary, and reactive feelings that appear in your mind and heart. The mindful moment with the sunset is any moment when you are present and your attention is focused upon the direct experience of what is happening as the sun sets. You are attentive and receptive, watching the changing light and colors and hearing the different sounds flowing through the moment. And when you notice your mind is beginning to comment or judge, you don't get lost in those thoughts, but let the thoughts go as you kindly bring attention back to the immediate, changing experience of the sunset in front of you.

The many simple moments of mindfulness come from what some people call our "natural" mindfulness. It is "natural" because it is part of being human, the same as having a body, or intelligence, or the capacity to feel and to give love. Like other human gifts, you can, with practice, more fully develop this natural capacity for noticing and being aware.

Moments of mindfulness are actually quite common. For example, when you notice the warmth of winter sunlight against your skin on a cold day, the moment of noticing the warm sensation is mindfulness operating. When you notice the sweetness in a bite of apple, the noticing of the sweet taste—before your mind takes off thinking about the apple (or something else)—is mindfulness functioning. Mindfulness is always operating here and now, in the present moment. And when you notice your mind is chewing over and over on some perceived injustice or some worrisome fear, or doing and redoing the same plan for tomorrow's activity, in that moment of noticing your thoughts or noticing the fact that you are stuck in a pattern of angry or fearful thinking, your mindfulness is operating. Mindfulness is *not* thinking, but instead is the awareness that recognizes your thoughts as they unfold.

Jon Kabat-Zinn, the father of mindfulness-based stress reduction (MBSR), puts it this way: "Mindfulness means paying attention in a particular way: on purpose, in the present moment, and nonjudgmentally. This kind of attention nurtures greater awareness, clarity, and acceptance of present-moment reality. It wakes us up to the fact that our lives unfold only in moments" (1994, 4).

As your life flows constantly through the present moment in ever-changing patterns, you can learn to be more steadily mindful—that is, to be more mindful of the conditions within you (sounds, feelings, thoughts, or bodily sensations, for example) and conditions around you (the specific context, other people, the environment, for instance). The result of learning to be steadily mindful can include remarkable clarity because you have gained the power of undistracted attention to illuminate previously unsuspected details about what is here and what is happening in the present moment. Because of this greater presence and focused, undistracted attention, you can experience a sense of deeper connection in any moment and a radical personal transformation in your understanding of and relationship to both the smallest things in your life as well as the bigger things. For example, in the earlier example of returning home from a busy day at work, being more mindful could help you see or hear more clearly loving joy or subtle upset in your child or partner. You might in turn feel yourself responding to that feeling, with the result being that both of you enjoy a more positive moment of deeper connection and understanding.

Meditation teacher Christina Feldman captures this amazing power of mindfulness to bring us more intimately into contact with our life. Describing a time when she taught a retreat in a desert community, Feldman noticed that, as her retreat days passed and she found time to walk in the desert, "I discovered that the more I looked, listened, and felt, the more I saw... It was a wondrous, alive, shifting, changing reality, different in each moment of the day." She goes on to say, "For anything in this world to be alive for us, we are asked to be alive to it. Mindfulness awakens not only our way of seeing, but also everything that is seen. If we look carefully at anything that we take for granted, we understand that it is the power of mindfulness which allows us to see it with new eyes, to be taught by it. It is only our concepts and images that stay the same, not our lives" (2001, 171–172).

In the past few decades, interest in mindfulness has grown exponentially in the Western world. Researchers in Western medicine and science, especially neuroscience, have found intriguing correlations between ancient wisdom about mindfulness and the modern understanding of changes in health and brain and body function. These benefits include research that directly supports mindfulness practice for calming and understanding anger and other destructive emotions. Here are some examples: mindfulness research now reports benefits for reducing stress (Kabat-Zinn 2013); facilitating changes in brain function correlated with increased feelings of happiness and well-being (Davidson 2012); improving emotion regulation and emotional intelligence (Goleman 1997, 2003); improvement of chronic depression (Williams, et al. 2007); and building capacity to experience positive emotions and to handle challenging situations (Fredrickson 2009).

These benefits came to people when they actually practiced mindfulness. Mindfulness is best understood, and has its most potent effects, through direct experience in the mind and body of the person practicing. This book is all about practicing mindfulness, and you will learn much more about that in later chapters. But before we get to that, let's take a closer look at anger itself.

A CLOSER LOOK AT ANGER

Mindfulness can definitely help you look more closely at you anger and, by doing that, help you take back control of your life from your anger and related feelings like irritation, rejection, and dislike. There are a few things you might notice when you take a mindful look at your anger: anger is made of thoughts and bodily sensations; anger, fear, and fixed ideas or beliefs are related to each other; and there are common misunderstandings about anger. Let's take a closer look at each of these now.

Anger Is Made of Thoughts and Bodily Sensations

On any list of the basic human emotions, you will probably find anger. Among researchers and psychologists, there is wide agreement that emotions are made up of more basic building blocks: the thoughts in your mind and sensations or feelings in your body. Anger is like this—it is made up of particular thoughts and sensations in your body. Specifically for anger, authorities generally agree that the perception you have of an event—that is, what you tell yourself about what is going on and what it means—determines whether or not anger will arise and whether or not your body will experience the resultant stress reaction that prepares it to freeze, fight, or flee from perceived danger. The key to understanding and mastering your anger rests in large part in your becoming more aware of both the thoughts you have and the sensations in your body whenever you feel angry. For example, think about how you might respond if you are waiting in line and in a hurry. You may notice some degree of bodily tension and impatience, but what happens in your thoughts can make all the difference in whether your tension and impatience become raging anger or they cool off, leaving you more at ease. How? Think about what happen if, feeling the tension and impatience, you become lost in thoughts like *I will never get out of here! This store is understaffed! These people don't realize how important it is for me to hurry up and be finished here, and they are in my way!* Having those angry, judgmental thoughts will feed more anger, and signal your body that there is more danger. Your body's stress reaction will become even more intense.

On the other hand, say you look at the line, feel the tension in your body and the impatience in your mind, and begin thinking, *Oh well, this is just how it is today. I can still get everything done. I am sure each one of these people would like to be out of here faster, just like I would.* Having those types of inclusive, friendlier thoughts, or shifting to them when angry thoughts appear, will signal to your body that there is little or no danger in this situation, and your body will begin to shift out of the stress reaction. You can see from an everyday experience like this one of waiting in line how the sensations in your body can combine with certain types of thoughts to produce the powerful emotion we call anger!

The Structure of Anger: A Helpful Map

So, if anger is basically particular thoughts plus particular physical sensations and reactions in your body, here is an additional perspective that you might find helpful: Imagine a three-level vertical relationship among anger, fear, and fixed ideas or beliefs, with anger on the top level, fear in the middle, and ideas and beliefs on the bottom level. The three are interconnected and communicate with each other constantly across the three levels.

It could work like this. Anger arises when fear is present. Fear comes out of a belief (or idea) that we are being threatened—physically, psychologically, personally, or in some other way. You could call this description of anger *the structure of anger,* because it represents the way anger is built on a lower foundation of fear, which rests on a still lower base of fixed beliefs or ideas. Anger does not arise without the non-anger factors—that is, without fear and fixed ideas or beliefs.

The structure could look like this:

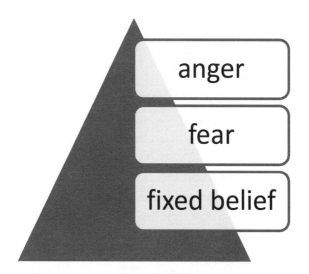

Here is an example. Jennifer is a student in a mindfulness class. She told the class the following story: "My girlfriend met me for lunch, and told me her boyfriend just proposed to her and they are going to be married. My first reaction was a feeling of shock, then I felt myself becoming upset and angry. Of course I congratulated her, but my tone of voice gave me away, and she asked if I was okay. I downplayed it, but I found a reason to leave early and went home. I was still pretty angry and wanted to understand my reaction more, so I took some time for meditation and began mindful breathing. I noticed where the anger was in my body, how my throat was hot and my jaw was clenched. I looked more deeply and could feel fear as a kind of shaking in my arms and legs. Listening closely, I could hear worried thoughts that were scary. They were telling me things like *You'll never get married. No one would marry you.* I listened more and questioned the thoughts mindfully: *Why do you say that?* I then heard the belief; in my mind, a voice said very clearly, *You are not a good person. You are not lovable.* I knew instantly that I have carried that belief about myself for all of my life." Jennifer said she was still upset, but she knew what she had to do. She talked to her friends and her therapist about the old belief that she was neither lovable nor a good person. In time, she began to change and to challenge the idea with more positive truths about herself. She enjoyed her friend's engagement and eventual marriage, and was able to heal her own pain.

Here is another example. John is a busy, hardworking man who has been feeling the pressure of a big project deadline on his job. He came to the mindfulness class because his doctor told him he had high blood pressure and needed to reduce his stress. One night he told the class this story: "I was on the job and stressing about my project one day this week. I had planned to stay late at work, when my buddy came to me and said he needed my help because his daughter was very sick and was being taken to the hospital. Basically, he asked me to take over his work for the rest of the day so he could leave early for his daughter. Immediately, I felt myself starting to heat up. 'Okay,' I told him, but I must have seemed angry, because he asked if I was sure it was okay. I was really mad then, and probably yelled at him to go on and get out of there. He shook his head, said thanks and that he owed me, and then left. I didn't like feeling that way, and started worrying about my blood pressure. So, I took a time-out and started breathing mindfully, just like we learned in class. As I calmed down a little, I started to notice what else was happening inside me. When I listened more closely to my worried thoughts, I could hear the angry words, *That's it, now you won't finish the project. You will be a failure.*" Suddenly, John became aware that he hated even the *idea* of failure, and believed that failing at anything was never an option for him. This gave him a new understanding of his fear of failure. John said he then questioned his belief that he could never allow himself to fail. *Why can't I let myself fail once in a while?* he asked himself. *What is so bad about "failure" anyway?* He admitted he knew he had plenty of time in the days ahead to finish the project, and he was actually ahead of schedule for his deadline. When he reminded himself of that, he felt his body relax and the anger fade. He was able to check in later with his friend, ask about the sick daughter, and smooth things out between them. John also told the class that failure was a lifelong fear of his, and seeing it arising again so clearly with his friend bothered him. He wondered if it was one reason his blood pressure was so high. He became more determined to focus on understanding the source of that fear, and to know where his beliefs about failure came from and the reasons those beliefs were so strong. John said he was now confident about understanding, and eventually beating, the fear of failure he had known his whole life.

Of course, this structure of anger model may not always be so immediately clear and informative in moments of anger. However, learning to look deeply and mindfully for the fear beneath the anger, and the beliefs or ideas fueling the fear, can be very helpful in disarming anger's power over you.

Some Misunderstandings About Anger

A common misunderstanding is that anger is a "hard-wired" instinct in human beings. But anger is not biochemically predetermined in us, nor is it instinctual. A possible threat arises, but you are not "wired" to be angry about it or to respond with anger. For that to happen, your mind has to analyze and decide that the possible threat really is a threat, and then mobilize a pattern of learned behaviors to drive an angry response rather than something else. You could say the arousal and alerting reaction in body and mind is wired into us as a protective reaction against possible threats, but the response following the arousal is complex and involves many reactions related to how you have learned to think and understand yourself, your feelings, and your interactions with others. For example, say you are walking down a street and a woman in front of you begins shouting and dancing about. Your first reaction could be one of alarm, and you may even jump back or find yourself immediately defensive with clenched fists, on hyperalert, and changing your bodily stance, preparing to fight or flee quickly. You may notice angry thoughts like *Someone should do something about people like this! They shouldn't be allowed here.* Suddenly the woman turns, and you see her face. You hear faint music, and you see she's wearing a pair of earbuds. At once, you realize she is simply absorbed in the music and moving to a favorite song, playing it loudly as she walks along—oblivious to everyone around her. Immediately you sense your body relaxing as you laugh to yourself, recognizing you are in no danger. You are no longer annoyed. What happened to your anger and fear once your perceptions of the woman changed?

Another misunderstanding about anger is that frustration automatically leads to aggression. How people respond to the inner feelings of frustration when they arise is very dependent on how they have been taught—or not taught—to take care of themselves and their feelings.

A third important misunderstanding about anger is the belief that one should always discharge or vent one's anger whenever it appears. Findings in modern neuroscience and psychology suggest that because our brains change depending on how we use them, it may not always be healthy to vent one's anger, because the venting just strengthens the tendency to become lost in angry thought patterns and reinforces the bodily reactions to those angry thoughts. The result of these repeated angry thought patterns and bodily reactions might be that in future moments, or similar situations, those same patterns of thinking (angry thoughts, for example) and stress reactions in the body could arise more quickly and strongly. Not reinforcing those patterns, conversely, can have the effect over time of the thought patterns actually quieting and fading—essentially cooling the emotion and helping the aroused body to restore calm.

THREE MINDFULNESS PATHS FOR TRANSFORMING YOUR ANGER

We all feel anger, and almost everyone suffers from anger at some time or another. This is no one's fault. We can't have everything we want. Life and other people can be frustrating and even hurtful at times. When anger arises in us, it always happens *now*—that is, in the present moment—and there are reasons and conditions that have come together in this moment that result in our feeling angry. By approaching your anger mindfully and with compassion, you can learn to touch that peaceful, enduring center within. As you view your anger from that center, you will find it easier to understand what causes your anger in that moment, to explore the deeper sources and building blocks of anger and pain in your life, and to better know how to heal your anger and to free yourself of its grip.

Earlier we mentioned that we would introduce you to three different paths, or approaches, that you could use to take back control of your life from anger and other strong emotions. These paths are built upon and reflect the wisdom of ancient mindfulness teachings as well as the perspectives of modern science and psychology, including the research findings mentioned earlier in this chapter. Countless people have followed one or more of these meditative paths and found freedom from destructive emotions like anger, and have learned to live with more joy, peace, and ease in their lives. It could happen for you, too! Here is a brief introduction to our three meditative paths for transforming your anger.

THE FIRST PATH: Disengage from your anger, pause to be mindful, and step back.

Like everything else that happens to us, anger appears and thrives in the present moment, in the here and now. Because anger arises so quickly and intensely, most of us don't even see it coming. How should we respond to this anger that comes so forcefully? What do we do now?

If you are in a burning building, the first order of business for you is to get out of that building! When anger burns you up inside, you can calm your angry mind by following the first path: disengage from your anger, become mindful of it, and step back from it. You may not be able to immediately stop the fire of anger, but just as when a building is burning, you can stop fueling the fire and avoid doing anything that will make the fire worse. Knowing you are angry and learning how mindfulness can help you disengage from it is your first path to calming your angry mind.

THE SECOND PATH: Cool your anger by using mindfulness and meditative practices to

nurture kindness and compassion toward yourself and toward others.

A remarkable insight about us as human beings is captured in this comment by the meditation teacher Sharon Salzberg, in which she encourages us to see love as an *ability*, not a commodity: "If we see love as a feeling, it is almost like a commodity—and likely we will judge our notion of that commodity all the time: 'I don't have enough, it's not the right feeling, it's not intense enough, it is too intense…' But if love is an ability, there is nothing to judge. As an ability, love isn't destroyed in the ravages of time and loss, insecurity, or disappointment. As an ability, love is always there as a potential, ready to flourish and help our lives flourish" (2008, 17–18).

Commodities can be spent or exhausted, but abilities can be improved and strengthened. Thinking of love as something that is not fixed, as something that can be developed and expanded, gives love infinite possibility, and this can be very motivating. For example many spiritual and wisdom traditions often speak of cultivating a heart of love and kindness for others, and also encourage us to include ourselves in that. This is reflected in the well-known instruction to "love thy neighbor as thyself." We see the power and wisdom of this when modern neuroscience informs us that our brains grow stronger in the ways we use them—and that activity in the circuits we don't use will fade.

Practicing mindfulness and meditations focused on cultivating kindness and compassion can benefit you by developing your innate ability to love and to be kind and compassionate. This is probably due in part to the fact that, by turning your mind intentionally toward kindness and compassion, you actually strengthen existing circuits and patterns in your brain. With these stronger circuits and patterns, you will be able to shift more quickly away from your anger into these stronger patterns of kindness and compassion. Making this shift prepares you for deeper reflection and insights into the causes of your anger, resentment, frustration, and pain. Thus, the second path calms your angry mind through mindfulness and meditative practices focused on kindness and compassion.

THE THIRD PATH: Practice mindfulness to transform your understanding. Realize that your anger is not an identity, a defect, or a permanent condition. To arise in the present moment, anger always depends upon specific other conditions.

The third path uses mindfulness to increase wisdom and understanding. Observing and mindfully reflecting on your anger reveals the true nature of that anger. You can see for yourself that anger is a changing and temporary emotion. After all, even when you feel intense anger, it doesn't last, does it?

Another critical point to understand about anger (or any emotion) is that anger is made from other conditions—such as distinctive thought patterns and specific bodily sensations—conditions that allow it to form and that feed its fire. Knowing that anger (and other strong emotions) are temporary, and depend on other conditions that you can observe directly by being mindful and come to better understand and transform, empowers you. Not only will you be less vulnerable, but you will also know and be able to take skillful actions to heal and transform the anger in your life.

These three paths or approaches—stopping and stepping back from anger, turning to kindness and compassion in the face of the pain and suffering related to anger, and becoming wiser about the changing, temporary nature of anger and how its existence depends upon other conditions of mind and body—have a strong basis in both ancient contemplative and spiritual traditions as well as in modern psychology and mental health approaches for mastering anger. This book and the practices we offer here invite you to explore these paths with mindfulness and meditation, and see for yourself how they can benefit you in dealing with your anger.

Mindfulness is the capacity you already possess for knowing and for being aware in the present moment. If you wish to cultivate the healing power of mindfulness in your life, and are willing to make mindfulness practice an important part of your life for dealing with anger or for any other reason, you have to be prepared to bring your whole being to the process. Practicing mindfulness practice is not simply a matter of mechanically following a set of meditation instructions and expecting something to happen. The power of mindfulness arises when you bring the dynamic living quality of your human intelligence and heart to the moment-by-moment unfolding process of mindful attention. The attitudes and intention you bring to any mindful practice or mindful moment are critical to this process. Let's take a closer look at the important qualities of intention and attitudes in mindfulness practice.

INTENTION AND ATTITUDE: THE KEYS TO BUILDING YOUR MINDFULNESS PRACTICE

Practicing mindfulness means choosing to be mindful. It means making a full commitment to being present and watchful in this moment, the present moment. It does not mean running after some special feeling or insight, nor does it mean trying to become someone else—like the "perfect" mindful person!

Practicing mindfulness is not forced at all. It is about inviting yourself to be present in full awareness in this moment, as best you can, and trusting that you already possess all you need to be mindful. When, in the moment, you intend to be mindful and pay attention with heartfelt curiosity and without judgment, you are practicing. The intention, motivation, and attitudes you bring to practicing mindfulness in any moment will make all the difference in the quality of mindfulness and your experience of being present and seeing clearly. Here are some essential attitudinal factors that will support you and help you build your mindfulness practice.

Intention. Commitment to practice is critical. Having the intention to be mindful for even one breath or one step helps provide the focus of energy and effort you need. Knowing that others have benefited from mindfulness and that it can also help you will strengthen you in your intention and commitment to practice.

Motivation. Why do you practice? Remembering and revisiting this question often is very helpful, especially when you experience periods of doubt or difficulty in your mindfulness practice. You may want to write down the main reasons for your practice in your journal or some other place where you can easily return to them. From time to time, revisit and reflect on them as your mindfulness practice grows. There is also a wonderful paradox related to motivation. In mindfulness practice, the harder you try to make something happen, the further away it gets! So, while it is important to be clear about your motivation because it can help mobilize energy and support your practice, as you practice mindfulness, it also helps to put any goals you plan to achieve aside. For example, your motivation might be to gain better control over your anger. Once you are clear on your motivation, the best way to practice is to put that aside. Avoid becoming obsessed with constant checking and analyzing to see if your mindfulness practice is "working." If your motivation is about better anger control, just practice mindfulness and watch what happens.

Skeptical Curiosity. Curiosity can be a source of energy in your practice. Ironically, having an attitude of skepticism—that is, not being totally convinced that mindfulness practice is going to help you—can be helpful, too. Skeptical curiosity is a kind of middle ground between the attitudes of blind faith and jaded cynicism. Blind faith—entering practice convinced that mindfulness is some kind of magic bullet for you—is likely to lead to confusion and disappointment. Jaded cynicism—despairing that nothing can help you and not really giving mindfulness practice a chance—betrays your intention and motivation immediately, all but ensuring that your experience with mindfulness will fail. Skeptical curiosity, on the other hand, is a much more constructive way to approach mindfulness practice. It says, "I don't know if mindfulness can help me, but I am curious and am willing to give it my best effort."

Crucial Attitudes. In developing mindfulness-based stress reduction (MBSR)—a formalized training program for learning to practice mindfulness to reduce stress and enhance health and well-being—Jon Kabat-Zinn (2013) identified seven specific attitudinal keys crucial in cultivating and growing your mindfulness practice. These attitudes are to be cultivated consciously. As he points out, "It is only when the mind is open and receptive that learning and seeing and change can occur… The attitude with which you undertake the practice of paying attention and being in the present is crucial. It is the soil in which you will be cultivating your ability to calm your mind and to relax your body, to concentrate and to see more clearly" (19). Here we provide a brief summary of those seven key attitudes. They are not independent of each other. Each one leads to all of the others, and they rely upon and influence each other in each moment of practice. Please reread this section once you are engaged in your mindfulness practice to remind yourself, even for one mindful breath or a single mindful step, of the ways you might become open to and explore the vast territory of awareness waiting for you through your practice.

- Nonjudging. Judgments are nothing more than forms of thinking. We need them, but we can also be the prisoner of deep habits of judging, and judging is a critical component of anger. For example, if you have decided or judged that a coworker is not really smart enough or hardworking enough for you, you probably notice dismissive, angry feelings inside when you think about that coworker. You may not know the coworker well at all, but you have formed a judgment about him that is negative, and because of your negative judgments, you carry angry feelings. You probably tend to dismiss him abruptly or even harshly when he approaches you with a new idea. Practicing nonjudging can be done by choosing to not to create more judging thoughts. An important part of that is not to be judgmental about having judgments! When you are mindful of the presence of judgments in your mind, the practice is simply to notice them, and perhaps name them by saying "judging" or "Judging thoughts are present." When you are not judging the judgments, you are actually practicing nonjudging.

- Patience. Patience is the capacity to bear difficulty with calmness and nonreactivity. Patience is born of wisdom—the wisdom that accepts that things change at their own pace. Impatience, which you are probably familiar with, is the opposite. Impatience is born of judgments. You may have noticed that when you are impatient, you have decided you want something different from what is happening here and now. So, you negatively judge the present situation—THIS is not good enough! You feel impatient—you reject what is here now and demand change. You are painfully frustrated in your attempts to control whatever is happening in this moment. Patience is not impatient! Patience is rooted in wisdom, kindness, and compassion. Patience knows things take time and have a life of their own, even the things we don't like and wish to change. Every time you mindfully recall that things always change and that, for everything, change happens in its own time, patience supports your mindfulness. Being patient helps you stay focused and attentive, bearing and understanding the pain of frustration. Patience also allows you to pause, rest, and heal the pain of your own impatience as you touch that pain with kindness and compassion.

- **Beginner's mind.** The Greek philosopher Heraclitus once said, "No man ever steps in the same river twice, for it's not the same river and he's not the same man." The truth of change is everywhere. The river flows constantly, and the water you step into now is not the same water that will be there one minute, or even one second, later. But, for different reasons, our minds like to ignore the truth of change and to create thoughts such as, *Just another river. I know what that is like. I've stepped in a hundred of them.* Assuming you already know all there is to know about this experience actually filters and blocks both the direct perception and the capacity to appreciate with wonder the fresh richness associated with what is happening to you right now. *Beginner's mind* is a crucial mindfulness practice attitude because it reminds us that each moment and what is here now is truly unique. Operating from beginner's mind means relating to the experience of this moment with freshness—as a true beginner who has not seen or felt any part of this experience before. Practicing with beginner's mind can help you dive deeply into the richness of this moment. Beginner's mind enables you be mindful and smell the rose right in front of you as if it were the first time, even if it is the thousandth time you have stopped to sniff a rose.

- **Trust.** Crucial to any moment of mindfulness is the basic trust that you have what it takes to know what is happening. Trust is the confidence in yourself that you, and only you, are the best person to know what is going on inside your heart, mind, and body in any moment. Trust is also the confidence that you have what you need already—the capacity for being mindful—to know with increasing detail and sensitivity exactly what is going on. Trust also helps you to be patient, as when you notice impatience is present and trust that you are capable of remaining attentive and open to the changing experience without having to act on it. By trusting in yourself that you do have what it takes to remain mindfully present in each moment, no matter what the moment contains, you will find what freedom from anger or other suffering means for you.

- Nonstriving. You may have heard the expression "Be quick but don't hurry." Hurrying is striving. When you strive, you lean forward toward something that you have decided cannot wait and that must be here now, and you reach impatiently for it. When you are caught up in striving, your focus is more about making the present situation go away or be finished than it is on doing things carefully and correctly. You can notice the sensation of striving in your body as a feeling of tension or gripping. You may hear striving thoughts in anxious voices in your mind as when you hurry through a task, not fully present, make mistakes and have to go back and correct them because the loudest thought you hear is *Hurry up and finish!* instead of *This is important, so take your time.* Nonstriving means dropping the reaching, suspending the judgments that drive the urge to fix or change what is here, and relaxing into being with what is happening. The paradox of meditation is that the real insights and benefits come when we stop trying to change anything or create any benefit. If striving is about dissatisfied and impatient "doing" (hurrying), then nonstriving is about wise "being"—letting things be as they are, even while you are working toward an important goal.

- Acceptance. In terms of practicing mindfulness and meditation, acceptance is the willingness to see things as they are. Until you are willing to stop and actually allow yourself to see what is happening or to feel it in your body, you will not really know what is going on; nor will you be capable of making real and lasting changes in your life. So when we refer to "acceptance," in mindfulness language, we are not saying you have to like what you notice, but we are saying it is important to let yourself actually see it completely and fully as it is, without denying or turning away if you don't like it or if something about what you are noticing and knowing is frightening or unsettling.

- **Letting go.** Have you ever noticed how your mind can tighten and hold on to a thought, feeling, or situation and not want to let it go, instead holding it close as you move through the changing conditions of your daily life? And, if you pay attention closely enough, you may be able actually to feel how your body joins your mind and grips with clenched teeth, tight fists, or tension in your shoulders or elsewhere. For example, if you are angry or not satisfied with how things are going in a relationship, your mind probably offers you some magical idea of what you "should" do to fix it, and you might find yourself stuck on that idea as you go through your day or week. The narrow, locked-in focus in your mind on that idea and the actual physical tension of holding on tightly in a region of your body when the idea is present could become so distracting that you would like all of the gripping tension to stop, but how? Our minds and bodies can easily be caught in this gripping, and for that reason, a crucial attitude in mindfulness practice is letting go. In the mindfulness-based practice, we notice when we are clinched and hardened (in mind and body) around a thought of any kind and make our experience of clinching and hardening the primary focus of our mindful attention. As we do this, we are letting go. We simply observe mindfully how each of these conditions—beliefs, judgments, indeed, any kind of thoughts, and the physical sensations that associate with them—arise in the present moment, and how each one comes and goes. So, letting go of the magic relationship solution might mean, in the meditation, that we notice the idea has appeared, but we don't add more thoughts of any kind to it. We just notice the idea that is here, stop holding onto it, let it go, and direct attention back to our focus—mindful breathing or the sensations of walking, for example. Sometimes letting go really means "letting be." In this case, in the meditation, if the magical relationship idea is very demanding, you may perhaps notice that "loudness" in the thoughts, not trying to change it or to be rid of it, but watching and letting it be. You watch and listen, mindfully present and noticing how the gripping and demanding idea changes, along with the bodily sensations that associate with it. If letting go or letting be is difficult, we can direct our attention more patiently and closely to the parts of ourselves that are holding on so fiercely. What do they say, and where are they in the body? For example, what is the tone of voice of expounding the magical relationship idea? Can you listen more carefully, just hearing the voice? Or, where in your body is the gripping happening—your jaw, fists, stomach, or someplace else? Bring kind attention to the sensations, and gently watch. By letting these parts "be" as they are as we direct mindful attention to them, they can teach us a great deal more about the process of letting go and where we tend to be stuck.

A QUICK LOOK AHEAD

Now that you have a basic understanding of mindfulness, anger, and the three mindfulness paths for transforming your anger, let's look at what lies ahead. In chapter 2, to explore each of the three paths in detail, you will learn seven core meditations for building specific skills to help you practice mindfulness. You don't have to master every core meditation, but we recommend that you at least try them all! Move at your own speed, and work with the ones that call to you most strongly. They are there to support you in strengthening your natural mindfulness. You don't have to be angry when you practice; just using the practices in your day-to-day life can be very helpful in freeing you from the grip of anger and transforming your life from one controlled by anger to one filled with joy and ease. Each of the core meditation practices is quite powerful, and any one of them, if you work with it, can help you become happier, more peaceful, and more present. We encourage you to make one or more of the core practices a regular and frequent activity.

In chapters 3 through 6, you will find a variety of mindfulness-based practices anchored in the three paths, and supported by the core meditations, to help you control anger and live more happily with your body, in your relationships, in your work life, and beyond. You can experiment with the core meditations in chapter 2 while you explore the other practices throughout the book. You don't have to master one before moving on to a different mindfulness-based practice. You will probably find that they support each other, and that your experience with any single mindfulness-based practice will enrich and inform your experience with any other.

We warmly invite and encourage you to move past this opening chapter on mindfulness to experiment and explore each of three meditation paths directly by using the mindfulness-based practices throughout this book. Only by your direct practice experience can you truly see for yourself how mindfulness can calm your angry mind.

KEEP IN MIND

Human beings are born with the potential to be mindful. You can be mindful of any experience and have probably had many mindful moments already. Mindfulness is the capacity and function of your mind that knows and accurately reflects what is happening now, in the present moment.

Anger and related emotions like irritation, frustration, ill will, and rejection are formed from combinations of thoughts and bodily sensations. You can learn to penetrate the veil of anger's illusions, and heal and transform the suffering that anger causes, by following any of the three paths or approaches based in meditative wisdom and modern psychology. Practicing mindfulness is critical if you wish to follow any of these paths of meditative wisdom, and practicing mindfulness requires a strong attitudinal foundation, with clear intention and motivation.

We wrote this book with the intention that it would provide you with the knowledge and guidance you need to build a personal mindfulness-based meditation practice. You can then use your mindfulness practice to reconnect with your wholeness, live more happily and peacefully, and better understand and manage anger in your life.

CHAPTER 2

Daily Meditations for Practicing Mindfulness

Human beings practice being mindful because they find they can be happier, live with more ease, and experience greater clarity and sense of purpose when they are more present for the moments of their lives and more present for themselves in each moment, regardless of what they are feeling or thinking.

Your natural ability for mindfulness grows much stronger and more available if you practice meditation. It may help to think of mindfulness as a capacity or talent for being present and aware. You were born with this capacity or talent; and like other human capacities and talents, mindfulness can be nourished and strengthened through consistent practice. So, it is important to take time to practice being mindful. We call this time "meditation." Interestingly, as we use the term, "practicing mindfulness meditation" does not mean rehearsing or trying to change anything. Practicing mindfulness meditation means simply noticing without judgment, without trying to make anything else happen, and without trying to become someone different from who you already are.

It is a paradox of mindfulness practice that we aren't trying to change anything or get anywhere; instead, we are practicing being nonjudgmental and more attentive, open, and aware of what is happening moment by moment. So, you might think of mindfulness meditation as the time when you pause—on purpose—and pay attention nonjudgmentally. That's it. Just stopping and noticing. Just watching without judgments.

Many different meditation methods or practices exist to help nourish the essential skills that support mindfulness—skills like building a steadier focus of attention or a less judgmental attitude but it is probably most helpful if you do not try to "develop" anything as you practice meditation. Instead, simply trust that by engaging in any of the meditation practices with curiosity, your mindfulness practice will be just fine!

In this chapter, you will learn more about mindfulness and practicing meditation as well as the basic qualities and essential skills of meditation practice that can help you discover the real power of mindfulness in your life. You may wish to refer back to this chapter from time to time for review as you explore the various mindfulness-based meditations and reflective practices in later chapters, or when you have questions or concerns about your experiences with those meditations.

EMOTIONAL BEINGS IN AN EMOTIONAL WORLD

We are emotional beings who live in an emotional world. Caught in the raging currents of emotional highs and lows, and tossed about by the many, often confused and complicated cultural messages about emotions like love, hate, and everything in between, it is easy to fall victim to the incorrect assumption that the world—in all of its changing display of appearances, expressions, and intensities—holds the ultimate power to make us happy, or to enrage and depress us. It is easy to be unhappy and confused, living without a deeper understanding of this world of emotions. When the emotions are painful ones, like anger, scorn, and rejection, it is also very easy to lose our sense of wholeness, the feeling of connection with others, and our deep knowing that all things are related and that we are always held within a complex and finely balanced web of life.

And yet people are very different when it comes to emotions. Have you ever noticed how some people become lost in an emotional moment while others are remarkably present and undisturbed in the same situation? Where does that presence and equanimity come from? Can anyone find it? Could that peace and ease be yours? Could you somehow learn to be present, resting in mindful stillness, and also be totally in contact with, acutely responsive, and knowing the feeling of any emotion?

We are not failures when emotions blind us. Who has not felt angry, alone, and more isolated as anger and ill will grow stronger? We are only human, after all. The good news is that no one has to remain blind, feeling lost, alone, or out of control because of intense emotions.

In this book, a guiding principle is that practicing mindfulness and meditation will help you both to manage your anger and other strong emotions more effectively and to live a richer and more rewarding life. Practicing mindfulness and meditation has helped many others to live with more peace and ease as well as learn to meet any situation more skillfully and with greater equanimity. It can help you, too! The core meditations in this chapter can help you experience the power of mindfulness, whatever your motivation.

YOU HAVE TO CHOOSE MINDFULNESS AND MEDITATION

At its heart, meditation is simple. It is about stopping the constant busyness, fixing, and planning, and just being here, now, and noticing. In mindfulness as formal meditation, or in any mindful moment, we stop and pay attention—relaxed, observing, being present with acceptance—and simply notice what is here. Turning to mindfulness is always a choice, but you have to make that choice. You have to choose for yourself to be mindful by how you pay attention in any moment.

Turning toward stillness and pausing to rest in awareness are not what most people choose when waves of emotion sweep through them in the present moment. There may be several reasons for this. One reason is that many people simply do not know there is an alternative to being swept away by emotion, or they do not know how to access that alternative. Another reason can be a lack of understanding about the nature of emotions and their deep link to the thoughts and beliefs we carry within. Or, some people have the mistaken idea that meditation is passive and can make them passive, but passivity is not what we mean by turning to stillness or resting in awareness. We are talking about opening ourselves to an experience of powerful presence that is always available to us.

Modern neuroscience has found that the ways we use our brains actually shape both how the brain functions and the brain structures themselves. Much evidence now exists confirming that training your mind by practicing mindfulness and meditation does actually change your brain. Practicing mindfulness is critical because the changes it brings—both to your brain and in your heart and mind as openings and insights—happen through the direct experience of being present with awareness, not by simply having more ideas about what is happening.

So, instead of blaming or locating responsibility for your peace and ease someplace outside yourself, by practicing mindfulness and meditation, you can tap into an experience of clarity, peace, and stillness within that you were previously unaware of. As you learn to touch the peaceful, enduring center within and draw upon that as a source of power to meet the challenges of the world, you may find that that place is always close, always here, gently present and waiting for you to notice it. And resting in that peaceful, enduring center could be simpler than you think—though it's not always easy!

BUILDING YOUR ESSENTIAL SKILLS WITH CORE MEDITATIONS

In this chapter, we will introduce you to and offer instructions for seven core meditations for practicing mindfulness. Each is powerful, and, as you will see, each offers a path for exploring the vast territory of awareness and increasing your ability to inhabit that territory. The meditations differ in emphasis and form, but ultimately they all point to the same place of awareness. Take your time with them. Practice with the ones that call to you. Relax and enjoy the support and experience of any of these core meditations that you like. You will probably find that these core meditations support the specific meditation practices appearing later in this book, so feel free to come back to any one of these whenever you like. If you wish, one or more of these meditations can become a daily meditation and be at the heart of your personal mindfulness-based meditation practice.

Practicing these core meditations will help you develop three essential meditative skills that are critical to deepening your experience of mindfulness: (1) training steadier and more flexible attention, (2) intentionally touching and cultivating qualities of kindness and compassion, and (3) engaging in mindful reflection concerning two important characteristics shared by all living things—impermanence and interdependency.

Developing these essential skills will also be very useful to you any time you work along one of the three meditative paths for managing anger that we introduced in chapter 1. You may recall that those mindfulness-based paths (or approaches) are stopping and stepping back from anger, turning to kindness and compassion to cool your angry reactions, and practicing mindfulness to transform understanding about your life and the nature of strong emotions like anger.

The seven meditations we share with you in this chapter are also "core" meditations because building the skills emphasized in these meditations can both open you to dimensions of human experience perhaps only dimly felt and add profound depth to your mindfulness-based meditation practice. For thousands of years, meditation teachers and students have practiced to develop the essential meditative skills of attention, kindness and compassion, and insight and understanding. They developed their meditative skills with practice, and you can, too!

Just a reminder: *It is important that you actually take some time and practice with these meditations! Give yourself the opportunity to experience mindfulness and meditation instead of just thinking more about it. Remember that your brain changes in response to how you use your mind to train it. You have to train your mind in meditation so that your brain knows which connections and circuits to build and which ones to allow to fade.*

The seven core meditations that we present here are not the only meditation practices that can build each essential meditation skill. If you know and prefer other meditation practices to train attention, grow compassion, and deepen understanding and wisdom through mindfulness, please use those! The instructions for the core meditations presented in this book can be used by all regardless of their level of experience with meditation and mindfulness. These meditations are designed to be simple and easy to follow. They may be used for formal meditation periods, or informal meditation in the flow of daily life—that is, when you decide to practice being mindful with what is happening in the present moment, including when you experience anger.

Take your time and work with these core meditations in any way you like. Pick any one that calls to you, or focus on the meditations for cultivating the particular meditative skill that you feel drawn to. You don't have to master them all, or even one of them, to feel the benefits of practicing with them. You don't even have to like a particular practice—just do it, giving it some time and perhaps a few tries before deciding anything about it. You can relax and allow yourself freedom to explore the vast territory of mindfulness as you experiment with these core meditations. Try practicing with an attitude of skeptical curiosity—not knowing what might happen but curious enough to give your best effort.

In fact, it will probably be most helpful if you actually forget about developing any skills at all or becoming different in any way, and instead just take up any of the meditations without trying to make anything happen or to get anywhere other than where you already are. Just practice with trust in yourself—trying one or more out as your "daily meditation" and coming back to it as often as you like—and observe with acceptance to see what that meditation can teach you.

FIRST ESSENTIAL MEDITATIVE SKILL: train attention to be stronger, steadier, and more flexible

Core Meditation: Mindful Breathing

Have you noticed how easily you can become lost in thoughts, worries, reactions to situations as well as in strong emotions like anger and frustration? Well, we all are subject to being lost like that! And it will likely happen again, many times, to most of us.

In those moments of being lost, remember that you already have what you need. When you notice that you are lost in challenging feelings and thoughts, use this basic mindfulness-based meditation practice—mindful breathing—to center yourself back in the present moment. Mindful breathing will help you disentangle yourself from the net of urgent thoughts and strong feelings in which you are caught.

Mindful breathing is also called "awareness of breathing," and it is a powerful core meditation practice that you may want to explore in your periods of formal meditation. You can practice mindful breathing in any position your body is in. Here is one way to practice mindful breathing.

Instructions for Practicing Mindful Breathing

- *Give yourself fully to this moment and to your breathing. Relax and let go of the doing and the busyness, and simply allow yourself to rest in noticing the sensations of breathing. Resting in awareness, know the feeling of your body breathing, of its natural rhythm of changing breaths, each with its own sensations.*

- *Let your attention rest lightly at the place in your body where you feel the sensations of your breathing most easily. It could be your belly rising and falling, your chest expanding and contracting, or the air moving in and out at the tip of your nose or in your mouth.*

- *Don't worry about the last breath or the next breath. Don't worry about doing it "right" or doing it "wrong." Relax.*

Resting in awareness, place your attention on this breath. That is good enough. If it helps to focus, you can whisper quietly to yourself "in" when you feel the sensations of the in-breath and "out" when you feel the sensations of the out-breath. No need to say "I am breathing" at all. Leave the "I" out of it. Keep it simple: "in" and "out." When you notice the stillness between the breaths, you can silently and gently note that by whispering to yourself, "Stillness." When you don't need the noting anymore, just let it go, and continue to notice silently the in-breath, the out-breath, and the stillness between.

- *When your attention moves to thoughts or sounds or other places in your body, it is no problem. You have not done anything wrong. Your mind just moves. It happens to everybody. When you notice that your attention has moved off of your breathing, recognize that it just happens, and it is okay. Then gently return your attention to the place in your body where you can feel the breath sensations most easily. When thoughts draw your attention, you have not made a mistake. Simply notice the thought and return attention to your breath. In this meditation, you do not have to fight your thoughts or control them in any way. You can simply notice them and let them be. You don't have to argue with or add to your thoughts either. Just bring attention back to your breathing and let the thoughts go.*

- *Continue your mindful breathing for as long as you like.*

In doing this practice, what have you discovered?

Core Meditation:
Mindfulness of Your Body

Your body is always in the present moment, and practicing mindfulness of your body is an excellent way to disentangle from strong emotions like anger and to place yourself firmly in the present moment. So, what does mindfulness of your body mean?

Have you ever stopped to consider that you are living *inside* your body, just as much as you are using your body to get things done? We humans are embodied beings—our experience of this life comes through our senses and our experience of being alive in these bodies. And our bodies do so many amazing things to keep us alive that we are not usually aware of, yet how often do we notice? How often are we grateful? For example, how often are you thankful or even aware when you have chewed a meal without pain in your mouth? Or, how often do you ignore the breath of life flowing in and out of your nose—until you get a cold or the flu and breathing becomes difficult?

And because, moment by moment, we are largely unaware and unappreciative of the miracle of embodiment, we readily become angry and critical of our bodies. When we judge that our body is not strong enough, not flexible enough, not attractive enough, not healthy enough, or any of a thousand other "not enoughs," we often relate to our bodies with anger and other feelings like rejection, dislike, aversion, and frustration.

Practicing mindfulness of your body can help you develop a very different relationship with your body. It will help you discover the amazing experience of living with more awareness inside your body. Mindfulness of your body can also help you appreciate and feel gratitude for your body. Often, practicing mindfulness of your body can help you uproot any negative and harmful attitudes of anger and judgment you may have developed toward your body.

Here are two core mindfulness meditation practices to help you mindfully explore the miracle of embodiment. No matter how quickly or slowly you move, no matter where you are or what you are doing, you can be mindful of your body. You can do this as a formal meditation or as an informal meditation, by weaving more bodily awareness into your daily life.

Part I: Instructions for Practicing Mindfulness in a Resting Body

- *Take a few moments and pause for meditation. Take a comfortable position that supports your body and encourages wakefulness, not sleep. Kindly and intentionally, focus your attention on the flow of sensations in your body. Begin by noticing stronger sensations, like the feeling of heaviness of your body, the position of your hands or arms, the feeling of your feet on the floor, or, if you are sitting, the contact of your back against the chair. Steady your attention, letting it be soft and gentle and noticing the sensations. Relaxing and resting in awareness, let the sensations come to you. You don't have to move or make anything happen. Trust yourself to know the changing flow of sensations as it comes.*

- *When your mind goes to thoughts, sounds, or someplace else, it is okay. You have not made a mistake. Just notice that your mind moves and remember that it happens to everyone. Patiently bring attention back to your body, feeling the sensations and knowing that you are feeling each sensation as it appears. Noticing the sensations of heaviness, perhaps, or vibrations. Relaxing and noticing areas of tingling or areas of no sensation. Noticing sensa-*

tions of warmth and coolness, dryness and moisture when they appear.

- If it helps, whisper a silent notation or label to yourself as you notice the sensation—"heaviness," "vibration," "pulsation," "warmth," or "coolness," for example. No need to make it too complicated. Keep it simple. No need to create a thought like "I feel heavy." Leave "I" out. Rest in the knowing, lightly whispering your label for the direct sensation. If the labeling becomes too confusing or distracting, simply let it go and maintain all of your attention on the experience of direct and changing sensations.

- As an informal mindfulness practice, pause throughout your day and tune in mindfully to your body. Relax, dropping into awareness and letting yourself notice the sensations in your body. Let any discovery you make about your body guide you in how you move or what you do next.

Part II: Instructions for Practicing Mindfulness in a Moving Body

- Mindfulness has no speed limit. It can be practiced anytime when you bring mindful attention to the sensations of your body moving through whatever activity you are doing. A classic method of formal mindfulness practice for the moving body is walking meditation. Walking meditation is a very helpful practice for discovering the miracle of embodiment. You usually begin with very slow walking, then move on to explore what happens when your body moves at different speeds. You don't need to be able to *walk on your legs, either. People in wheelchairs frequently practice mindful "walking"—formally as they focus on the sensations in their body when they roll themselves back and forth on their meditation path, or informally as they go about their day's activities.*

- *As a formal meditation, walking meditation can be done by choosing a path of several steps (some recommend fifteen to twenty steps in one direction before turning around), placing attention on the changing sensations in your feet as you walk to the end, stop, turn, and walk back on your path. When you have thoughts or your mind moves some-place else, just notice without judgment and return atten-tion to your focus on the changing sensations of walking. In this practice of formal walking meditation, you cultivate mindfulness of the body by focusing on your walking body and not on walking to get someplace else. Walking medi-tation is an awareness practice, not a walking exercise!*

- *As an informal mindfulness practice, you can experiment with mindful walking, which means simply turning mindful attention to the experience of walking as you walk to get someplace. For example, you could practice walking mindfully in your home as you go from room to room, or where you work as you walk around; or you could prac-tice walking mindfully outside in a park or by the ocean. Walking mindfully means opening to your experience, noticing the sensations of walking, and anchoring your attention in those sensations, instead of becoming lost in planning or thoughts and judgments or emotions and memories about something else. Walking mindfully is a beautiful way to come back to your body and to connect with what is here in this moment.*

Core Meditation: Open Awareness

We live our lives in moments, and the present moment, this moment right now, is where it all happens. If we are lost in recalling the past or intensely planning or worrying about the future, our thinking is actually happening *now,* in this moment—even if the focus of our thinking is on the past or future.

Practicing mindfulness can bring you back to this moment and help you truly know and wisely relate to all that is here. Mindfulness means being receptive and openhearted toward all experience here, now. It means you don't leave anything out, which is very important if you want to understand clearly and effectively manage emotions like anger; deal with pain from grief, injury, or illness; or be open to the beauty and mystery that await you in each moment of this human life.

In many mindfulness-based practices, the instruction is to choose a primary focus for attention. For example, when you practice mindful breathing, you choose to focus on the sensations of your body breathing, and you return your focus to your breathing whenever your attention wanders. In mindful walking, you choose the sensations of walking as your primary focus for attention.

This core meditation is called *open awareness* or *bare attention.* It is also sometimes called *choiceless awareness* or *open presence,* because in this practice, we do not choose a particular single object as the focus for attention, but instead open our focus of attention completely to include equally all feelings, thoughts, and sensations—everything that comes into and passes through the present moment.

A popular metaphor for this mindfulness-based practice is to imagine that your mind is like the sky. Just as the sky contains many different things—clouds, birds, sunlight, and so on—your mind contains many different things—thoughts, feelings, sensations, and different sensory impressions. When practicing the open awareness mindfulness meditation, let your attention be as vast and open as the sky, and notice anything that arises rather than ignoring or rejecting it.

Another common metaphor for this practice is to imagine you are seated on a riverbank. Your attention is fixed lightly on the scene before you, which is only a small segment of the flowing river. As you watch, a variety of objects float by in front of you on the river; an object first comes into view, passes by, then floats out of your view. In open awareness, you can imagine you are sitting on that river watching, and the objects that float by are different sensations, sounds, images, smells, and tastes as well as all sorts of thoughts and feelings. The practice is just to observe each object with equal curiosity and friendliness until it floats away, then bring the same attention to whatever next floats into view.

Discovering the power of open awareness to bring mindfulness to the full expression of each moment can be startling. It also suggests not only that the territory of mindfulness is much vaster than we may have suspected but also that we are much more amazing and mysterious as human beings than we give ourselves credit for being.

Instructions for Practicing Open Awareness

- *For a formal practice, take some time for your meditation; put down other activities, assume a comfortable position, and let yourself drop into awareness.*

- *If you like, you can begin by mindfully focusing on your breathing or your body sensations. When you feel ready, shift from this focus to the practice of open awareness.*

- *Just sit with what is here, observing and allowing it to come to you, reveal itself, and pass away. You don't have to look for anything or restrict your focus. Just sit and watch. Being receptive, notice whatever comes into your awareness through any of your senses or your mind. Allow whatever you notice to be just as it is. Resting in awareness, notice with increasing sensitivity how each experience arises and fades away. Practice for as long as you like, stopping your formal meditation session when you are ready.*

- *As an informal mindfulness practice, experiment with pausing and practicing open awareness for brief periods throughout the day, in different situations. Let go of your agenda and pause to notice, even for a few breaths. In that moment, open your focus to all that is happening. Include everything and give everything equal attention, if only for a single moment or breath.*

SECOND ESSENTIAL MEDITATIVE SKILL: cultivate qualities of kindness and compassion

Core Meditation:
Developing Loving-Kindness

If you notice that the content and quality of your thoughts is often dominated by ill will, anger, and rejection of others, yourself, or the world in general, what can you do?

A traditional remedy in wisdom and spiritual traditions for feelings of anger, hatred, and rejection is to cultivate kindness and to do kind acts for others. This view has some support from modern neuroscience, which has found that circuits and connections associated with repeated thought patterns and feelings strengthen with use, and other circuits of brain activity wither and fade with disuse. Oversimplified, the message is this: if you want to feel kinder and less angry, do kind things for others and think kinder thoughts! Not always so easy, is it?

Recall what we said about anger in chapter 1. Anger arises as a sudden storm—you probably don't even see it coming until it has taken hold in your body and your mind. If, however, you pay closer attention, you may notice the feelings associated with being angry—the tension, gripping, and pounding heart, for instance. Looking deeper, you may begin to hear angry thoughts about the situation you are in—thoughts that are repeated over and over. If you find yourself stuck on a story of how someone has hurt you, and if you continue focusing your thoughts on your hurt and how you wish to hurt that person in return, then you strengthen those patterns of thinking in this moment. The next time you feel hurt by someone (even a different person), these angry thoughts and feelings will probably arise sooner and may even feel more intense. This is how your brain works. To change those feelings, you have to change the patterns in your brain. That can happen by training your mind in different patterns—patterns of greater awareness and kindness.

Here are simple instructions for practicing a core meditation—*loving-kindness*—to nurture your natural qualities of kindness and to strengthen those patterns and circuits in your mind and brain. One meaning of loving-kindness is "great friendliness." It could be the feeling we have for a person we care about, and it is expressed when we wish that person well without expecting anything in return—for example, as when a dear friend leaves on a trip and we say things like "Have a safe trip! Enjoy yourself! Be well!"

Many mindfulness teachers have observed that mindfulness without kindness is not mindfulness. Indeed, you may already have noticed that moments when mindfulness seems difficult are the moments when your mind is filled with anger or other harsh feelings. The anger and ill will may actually obscure what is happening in that moment, like some sort of smoke screen blocking your view of the other person, your surroundings, or what is inside of you. In those times, the core meditation practice of loving-kindness can help.

In this meditation, you will draw upon both the feeling of generous and freely offered kindness as well as wishes for well-being for yourself or others. As part of this, you will silently repeat simple phrases of well-wishing and friendliness to help you connect with your natural qualities of kindness and friendliness. This practice is about generating and sending good wishes; it is not magical thinking that maintains that somehow we are responsible for what happens to other people.

The phrases here are not the only phrases you can use, but you can start with them. The phrases you use should resonate with you. Also, loving-kindness phrases are best if they capture wishes for something that any person—indeed, any living thing— would be happy with. For example, you might use any of these phrases: "May you be happy," "May you be peaceful," "May you be healthy," or "May you be safe."

Instructions for Practicing Loving-Kindness

- *Whenever you like, pause for a few moments for formal meditation to practice loving-kindness. Assume a position that supports wakefulness and provides comfort to your body. Feel free to shift position at times, if it helps you stay present.*

- *Begin by practicing mindful breathing for a few moments. When you feel ready, shift to the practice of loving-kindness meditation. Recall any kindness and love you might have felt from a dear friend or family member. Or remember and let yourself feel the love of a small child when the child took your hand. Or remember the feeling of receiving the love of a pet, or the feeling you may have experienced in the beauty of nature as you viewed a majestic mountain or a tranquil lake, smelled a wonderful flower, or walked by a crashing sea, or anyplace else that comes to mind.*

- *Let this feeling of love and kindness fill you as much as possible. You don't have to force it or imagine anything. Trusting yourself and turning attention to any feelings you have of love and kindness, allow yourself to truly feel them. If you don't feel anything, that is okay, too. In this practice, it is the intention that is most important.*

- *Bring attention to yourself and begin whispering phrases of loving-kindness, wishing yourself well—just as you might, with great friendliness, wish a dear friend well if your friend were leaving on a trip. You could whisper something like "May I be happy," "May I be healthy," "May I be peaceful," "May I be safe." Choose a word or phrase that resonates for you as a genuine reflection of your heartfelt kind wishes. Other examples include "May I be joyful," "May I enjoy ease of well-being," "May I be protected from inner and outer harm," or "May I live with ease, free from worry.*

- *The classic form of this meditation also includes sending loving-kindness phrases to others. Shift your attention to a teacher, a loved one, a person you do not have strong feelings about, a difficult person, and to as many others as you like. Practice with these different types of other people, sending them loving-kindness individually during a meditation period, or, including them all in a single meditation period, moving slowly from one to the next, and returning to yourself at the end of the period of formal meditation. How you feel is as important as what you notice and how you maintain your intention to send loving-kindness.*

- *As an informal practice, try turning to loving-kindness for yourself or others in different situations throughout your day. Pause to repeat one or more phrases and direct them to yourself and to others.*

What do you notice when you shift your focus of kind wishes from one type of person to another? What do you notice when you turn to loving-kindness for yourself or others during your day?

Core Meditation: Developing Compassion

What do you do when, being mindful, you notice more acutely the pain in another or become aware of pain in yourself? Compassion is the strong wish of the heart to alleviate the suffering of others. Who isn't moved by the pain of a sick child or the despair of a starving refugee in a war-torn country seen on the evening news? This pain, when noticed, opens our hearts; we hear its call, and we are moved to act.

To view life with compassion requires us to be willing to stop and look at what is happening around us and inside of us. Compassion challenges us to keep looking, more deeply if necessary, at the conditions that give rise to it. It can take real courage and faith that we have what it takes to face pain with compassion, because being compassionate requires us to stay present with pain in any form, including our own feelings of fear and vulnerability. As we experiment with compassionate acts, and with meditations on compassion, we come to trust that we can eliminate our inner blind spots, befriend our own pain, and nurture the growth of compassion in our lives. We come to know with certainty that facing pain mindfully and compassionately will not destroy us.

As you experiment with compassion in your own life, when you feel yourself drowning in pain or getting lost in despair and fear as a reaction to pain and suffering, know that this is natural. Those feelings can be worked with. In those moments, you might turn back to your breath for stability and refuge; breathe mindfully, anchoring yourself again and again in the present moment. It can also help—as you breathe with awareness, mindful of your own despair and pain—to recall that you are not alone. All living things suffer, and the pain and the desire to be free of it is something that unifies us all. Finally, you may find strength in the truth of change and impermanence, reminding yourself that this pain, like everything else, is temporary and changing, even as you observe it compassionately.

Compassion begins when we are capable of seeing the pain in another, even if that pain is clouded by angry or hurtful words or acts. Compassion involves the wisdom to know how to act (and when not to act) to ultimately relieve the pain of another. Compassion requires the equanimity and strength to protect ourselves and to set and maintain appropriate boundaries. Compassion also means including the pain in ourselves as worthy of kindness and attention.

There are many ways to practice compassion meditations. Realistically, we know our sincere wishes for ease and relief of suffering will not cause pain and suffering to magically vanish. Yet we practice the meditations anyway. Meditations on compassion are meant to help us tap into our innate human capacity for goodness as well as to discover the wisdom and strength within to transform our way of relating to suffering. In the compassion mindfulness-based practice, we can find a means for opening to a tenderness of heart and strength of spirit that illuminate our connection with anyone who suffers, empowers us to help others and ourselves, and affirms that we are never alone.

Instructions for Practicing Compassion

- *As a formal meditation practice for developing compassion, you can begin by bringing attention to your breath for a few moments as you practice mindful breathing. When you are ready, and feeling present, shift your attention onto a real person to whom you wish to direct compassion. It could be someone you know who is enduring great mental, emotional, or physical pain.*

- *Remember that your practice is most importantly about intention and that your well-wishing may bring up a variety of feelings in yourself. Please meet any painful feelings you have within by breathing mindfully with them, holding all these feelings with awareness and self-compassion.*

- *Begin sending your compassion to the other person by silently and softly repeating phrases to yourself in a heart-*

felt way. Your phrases could be related to their condition, like "May you be free from the pain of your injury," or "May you find peace and ease in this time of grief," or "May you be free of the pain beneath your anger." Your phrases can also be more general, like "May you be at peace" or "May you find healing."

- When you feel ready, shift attention to yourself. Including yourself in the compassion meditation can come in phrases like "May I find peace," or "May I find the resources to befriend and heal this anger, this fear, and this pain," or "May I find the resources to view my limits with compassion, just as I view the suffering of others."

- If you wish, experiment with including different types of people in your meditation. You could practice sending your compassion to teachers, friends, people you don't know well or have strong feelings for, difficult people, and all living beings. Include anyone who makes sense to you. Imagine you are speaking to that person and choose a phrase that rings true for you. It could be something like "May you be free of pain and fear," "May you feel safe," or "May you live and die with ease."

- Let your own goodness and intelligence guide you in choosing your phrases. What do you notice as you practice compassion using your phrases? Let whatever you notice in yourself guide you.

- You can practice compassion meditations informally in moments of your life by turning to a favorite compassion phrase and silently directing it at another or toward yourself whenever you notice pain and suffering is present.

THIRD ESSENTIAL MEDITATIVE SKILL: recognize the characteristics of impermanence and interconnectedness as they unfold in the present moment

Core Meditation: Recognizing the Truth of Change, Moment by Moment

Life constantly flows through the present moment. If you stop and rest more often in your natural ability to be mindful, then you can actually see for yourself how rich, varied, and utterly temporary the conditions of this life truly are. For example, you may have recognized change when you noticed afternoon shifting into evening or when you noticed your coffee cup has changed from full to empty.

Impermanence—the changing nature of life experience that flows into and out of the present moment—also includes your inner life of thoughts, emotions, and bodily sensations. For example, you may notice your body position has changed from sitting to walking, or even that each foot changes from being on the ground to moving in the air as you walk, and the sensations in your body change with each of these movements. Constant change includes thoughts and emotions, too, as when you notice the thing you worried about so much yesterday has not happened and that you are not worried about it today.

Bringing mindful attention to the truth of change in every aspect of your experience can be a powerful source of equanimity that will help you manage anger and forms of disturbance in your life. Here is a meditation practice to support mindful reflection on change.

Instructions for Practicing Mindfulness of Impermanence

- *As a formal meditation practice, breathe mindfully for a few minutes and then turn your attention to the changing conditions of your breath. Notice how the in-breath has a beginning, a middle, and an end, and how a brief pause of stillness then follows the in-breath. Notice how the stillness changes into the sensations of the out-breath, which also has a beginning, a middle, and an end, and yields to more change and a new moment of stillness.*

- *As your meditation continues, let yourself notice how everything coming into awareness through your senses is changing. For example, focus on the sounds you hear. Can you hear the changing sounds as they come to you without being lost in the thoughts that arise about any one sound? Do you notice how the sensations flow and change throughout your body? Can you listen or observe how your thoughts are constantly changing, noticing how they appear, disappear, and have different tones of voice and degrees of urgency or ease?*

- *End your formal meditation with a reflection: What have you noticed about the depth and degree of change?*

- *As an informal practice, at times throughout the day, pause and breathe mindfully. Notice how things around you are changing. How do the things you are looking at change? How do the sounds that you hear change? Are the sensations in your body still changing? Your thoughts? Your moods? Pause and reflect whenever you wish on the deep and broad nature of impermanence.*

Core Meditation: Recognizing the Dynamic Web of Mutual Interdependence and Connectedness Holding Us All in Each Moment

Everything in this life depends on other conditions and elements in order to exist. For example, a rainbow forms in front of you while you water your lawn. For this to happen, the necessary elements—light, water, you holding the hose, and other factors— assemble in the present moment. If any of these elements (each of which is formed by other elements) is missing, the rainbow does not appear. For the rainbow to come into existence, different elements that are not rainbows must come together in a particular combination to create it. The rainbow only exists when all of these elements are present and join together. The rainbow is dependent on and connected to each of the elements, which are necessary for the rainbow to come into being. In this view, you can see that the rainbow is made of nonrainbow elements and deeply interconnected with them.

We give a specific name to the particular manifestation that is formed when a group of different elements (or conditions) come together in the present moment. In the example above, the name we gave that manifestation was "rainbow." And with the naming of a temporary manifestation of combined conditions, we give weight and importance to the thing that we just named.

Naming something is useful for many reasons, of course, and we do it all the time. But naming can be complicated, even risky, if we begin to assign too much meaning to being "right" about our "idea"—that is, the name we have given to the temporary aggregate of conditions or elements.

For example, we name a collection of apples, butter, spices, sugar, heat, moisture, and other ingredients "apple pie," but the name is simply a designation we apply to what is here when these different elements and conditions have come together temporarily. With the name, the thoughts and opinions begin. What makes a "good" apple pie or a "bad" one? Do people ever get angry and argue about their apple pies? Is it the actual apple pie they are arguing about or the idea they hold of what the apple pie should or should not be? Has being "right" about the apple pie become more important than the apple pie itself?

Seeing the interdependent, temporary nature of life directly with mindfulness can protect us from giving too much authority to our thinking mind's opinions and ideas and to our own feelings of righteousness about our ideas.

Anger and other emotions are like the rainbow and the apple pie—anger is the name we give to temporary (usually intense!) expressions of (perhaps not so intense) nonanger elements including perceptions, bodily sensations, and strong opinions and ideas. Observing mindfully, we can see that anger and other emotions are *real*—that is, here in this moment—and *not substantial*: that is, they are temporary and require many other elements to join together in order to appear.

Anger and other emotions flowing through this moment can be contagious, too. If my presence and action is one of the conditions arising in the present moment of your life, if I feel angry when I am around you, there is a good chance that I will do or say something that triggers or fuels anger, fear, or another strong emotion in you. This interconnectedness and interrelatedness is simply how things are for us as human beings. Our feelings, indeed our lives, are dependent in large part on interacting with each other. What values and intentions drive our actions and expressions in any moment as we flow in and out of relationships? How might we come into better alignment with our deepest values and live more wisely, with more ease and compassion?

Observing this flow of changing appearances in each moment, we can see that nothing is ever really isolated or separate. When we don't see this constant connectedness, it is not because there is no connection, but because our way of seeing has become obscured. Practicing mindfulness can be thought of as learning to see with new eyes. Present, awake, and observing with acceptance, we are ready to sense more clearly the connections and possibilities here in this life in each moment. Experiment with the following meditation to reflect more deeply on the nature of interconnection and interdependency.

Instructions for Practicing Mindfulness of Connection and Interdependent Conditions

- *Either as a longer formal meditation or in any moment of daily living, pause and take time to be mindful of the connectedness present in this moment.*

- *Place steady attention on your breathing or on mindful walking, if you like. When you are ready, look around. If your eye falls on a cloud, can you look deeply and see the elements of water, air, heat, light, and other factors that help it to appear? In your own noticing, can you include your eyes, your brain, and all that you are—all of which are also critical elements in making this moment of you noticing the cloud real? As your attention moves to something else, can you see how the moment of noticing the cloud has changed, because a key element—you noticing—has moved on?*

- *Practice noticing of the elements and your own consciousness changing in each moment as you look deeply and mindfully at other objects—buildings, steps, trees, flowers, animals, food, whatever you choose. You don't have to try. Just relax into awareness and observe. With your full attention, include what is happening in your own mind, heart, and body. Practice for as long as you like.*

As you practiced, what did you notice?

WORKING WITH THESE CORE MEDITATIONS

Here are some helpful suggestions for how you might make these mindfulness-based practices an important part of your life.

- *Take time each day for dedicated moments of stillness.* Stop your doing and fixing of things and simply allow yourself time to be. Take advantage of those times to practice any one of the core meditation practices as a formal meditation period.

- *Create a space for meditation.* It is important to support your intention to practice mindfulness and meditation by creating a space for your practice. Your space should be comfortable, have limited distractions if possible, and allow you privacy when you need it. Many people like to adorn their meditation space with one or more objects to inspire and support them. Photos of teachers, loved ones, or meaningful figures or objects from nature are popular. These are not necessary, but can be very supportive reminders that many others have struggled and benefited from meditation.

- *Create a time for meditation.* With so many other demands, you can easily lose time in your schedule for formal meditation periods. If you don't want that to happen, make appointments with yourself for meditation! Put them on your daily calendar. If you can, build your meditation period into the same time each day—for example, just before breakfast or just before going to bed. Making time for meditation is just as important as anything else you do to keep yourself happy and healthy. And, like eating, sleeping, or brushing your teeth, you have to make meditation a priority!

- *Make a personal commitment to informal and formal practice.* Formal practice happens when you pause to take time for meditation and put all other things aside. The amount of time you take is up to you, but what you are doing is practicing your meditation. Informal practice happens when you pause for even one mindful breath or step in the flow of daily experience and notice what is happening. You can pause to notice as often as you like. By making a habit of noticing, you will probably find that noticing comes more often. Formal or informal, the intention to practice and the personal commitment to practice are crucial. You don't have to like it—just do it!

- *Consider music, candles, and other supports.* Many people think they need music or candles to practice meditation. Actually, they don't. Mindfulness is about noticing, and you already have all you need: just choose to pay attention in the present moment without judgment.

- *Consider the effects of drugs and alcohol.* We practice mindfulness to wake up. Mixing alcohol or drugs with your meditation practice will ultimately work against you. Please get help if you need it if you have formed habits of using substances, and bring a clear mind and an open heart to your practice. It is also helpful to notice any side effects from prescribed medications, and, as best you can, allow for those when you plan your formal meditation. For example, if your medication makes you sleepy for a period of time, you may try and schedule your formal meditation when that side effect has passed.

- *Work with painful thoughts and unpleasant sensations.* To be mindful of any thought or sensation means to observe it with acceptance, not try to fix it or change it or to escape from it. Just be present and discover what it can teach you. Painful memories or doubts can be a hindrance to your practice, but they don't have to be. By recalling the core attitudes of patience and trust, and the simplicity of mindfulness—just watching with compassion and acceptance—you can turn toward any difficult thought or sensation. On the other hand, it can also help to give yourself permission to turn away or step back from the meditation at times if you don't have the energy or strength of attention to stay present with the difficult thought or sensation for a long period of time. The important thing is to keep your intention turned toward that which is difficult and seek to understand it, while being sure to practice the art of self-care and wisdom in each situation.

KEEP IN MIND

Practicing mindfulness in formal meditation and in any moment requires intention. You have to choose mindfulness; and practicing core meditations to build attention, kindness and compassion, and insight can help deepen and fortify your mindfulness practice, whatever your motivation, including to heal and transform the toxic pain of anger and other strong emotions.

PART 2

Meditations for Calming Your Angry Mind and Living with Greater Joy and Ease

CHAPTER 3

Calming Anger In or About Your Body

How often have you felt your body stiffen or harden in anger, or found yourself unable to relax because your body was so agitated from the heat of anger? How many times have you felt some form of anger or ill will toward your body? How often have you found yourself relating to your body as an enemy, instead of as a close and supportive companion in your life?

You may be angry for many reasons, but your angry feelings are based both in the complex relationship between your mind and body and in the constant interaction of bodily sensations, perceptions, strong ideas, judgments, and deeper fears that you carry within.

Perhaps your angry thoughts toward your body came from a belief that your body was not good enough, not pretty or handsome enough, too tall or not tall enough, or that your body was too fat or too thin. Perhaps you became convinced that your mind and brain didn't function correctly, and there was no hope for you.

Anger toward your body can also be related to fears you hold about your body. Many people feel angry, for example, when they are told they have an illness like diabetes or cancer, or when they suffer an injury. After the experience of illness or injury, they begin to feel deep fear about what illness or injury will mean for them.

Pain in your body can be a source of anger, too. Have you ever known anyone who became angry at the pain of a migraine headache, for example, or the pain of a toothache? You also may have noticed how easy it is to become angry at even mild discomfort in your body. For example, have you ever become irritated or angry at the unpleasantness of a common cold? Many people have!

Negative, angry, and worried thoughts in your mind can become a source of fuel that makes the pain worse. For example, some research links back pain with long-standing anger at others or a situation you feel helpless to control. Other research has found that some people interpret chronic pain as a kind of spiritual punishment. These people actually become worse emotionally and physically, which is perhaps linked to their growing despair over believing that they deserve punishment and cannot make amends.

Your body can become hardened and agitated by anger at another person, too. Or you may become caught up in anger toward a group of people or a situation that upsets or enrages you. This angry reaction in your body connects and interacts directly with the anger in your thoughts and feelings in that moment. The angry, hyperalert body can be uncomfortable, and it can become a problem when this hyperarousal becomes chronic and negatively impacts your health and relationships.

That angry reaction you feel in your body can be so intense that you carry it through your day. You might call it the "stress reaction" in your body because it involves the same physiological hyperarousal mechanisms of the familiar "freeze, fight, or flight" reaction. It can actually drive you to explode later in anger or rage at someone who has done little or nothing to deserve it! Has anything like that ever happened to you?

Whatever the source, the anger you feel in or toward your body can be transformed. There is always something else you can do—and only *you* can do it. You can change your relationship to your body and whatever you experience physically—anger, agitation, illness, injury, pain, aging— through mindfulness, compassion, and wisdom, which you can cultivate and nourish in any moment of your life.

Learning to turn toward mindfulness and compassion whenever you feel anger in or toward your body can help you engage one or more of the important mindfulness paths for healing and transformation (see chapter 1). For example, you can step back and stop feeding the angry thoughts. You can respond to your body's condition with compassion. You can deepen your understanding of the sources of anger inside you, seeing them as only temporary and fear based and realizing that your anger is not a personal identity but only a reaction. As you move along any of these paths, you will not only change your response in or to your body, but you will also greatly support and enhance the healing process your body requires. In essence, when your body really needs you—when it is sick or injured or in pain—instead of reacting with anger and making things worse, you can respond with mindfulness and compassion, and become a potent force in your own healing.

The mindfulness-based practices and exercises in this chapter are intended to help you use any of the three core approaches toward anger and to apply the path you choose to any feelings of anger, ill will, or rejection that you have in or toward your body or what you experience in your body. You may recall the three core approaches (or ways to relate to your anger) are (1) stopping and stepping back (or disentangling) from overidentification and involvement with anger, (2) intentionally shifting your response to one based in kindness and compassion in the situation where anger arises, and,(3) letting mindful attention to anger and its causes reveal new understanding and different responses in each situation where anger is present.

You may also recall that each of these three core approaches to anger are made more accessible as you develop the essential meditative skills of building stronger and steadier attention, touching your deep reservoir of kindness and compassion, and seeing clearly how the experience of strong emotions like anger is always impermanent and dependent on other factors. So, as you explore these practices, please remember that you don't have to wait until you are ill, injured, or in pain. Wisdom and compassion, as well as gratitude and appreciation, can be cultivated mindfully at any time toward any kind of body— healthy or ill, young or old, large or small.

Over the next few pages you will find nine body-centered mindfulness practices you can use in daily life. Choose any that call to you.

Learn to Really See Your Body

When you look in a mirror at your body or a part of your body, do you see what others see? Or do you see the body you remember from the past, an imaginary body you wish you had, or perhaps the image of a body you are afraid of or even angry about seeing?

Our minds operate so quickly that we may not realize that, moment-by-moment, they create an inner reality for us that combines immediate sensory input, memories from past experiences, and our ongoing thoughts, sensations, and emotions. What our minds create in our consciousness from this mix is not always an accurate representation of what is present before us.

For example, a thin person may look in a mirror and accurately see his body shape and lines. But then his mind adds images from the past, judgments, fears, and emotions to the visual input from the mirror image, creating a distorted internal perception. The result? The person "sees" a body that is too fat. Self-hatred and anger thrives on such misperceptions.

In another example, one person sees and goes to painful lengths to hide her artificial leg, while another runs in marathon races, proudly displaying and depending on her artificial leg. They both have artificial legs, but their inner views and perceptions of their bodies are quite different. These inner views and body perceptions drive their feelings and actions related to their bodies—and their resultant life experiences—in very different directions.

Your attitudes about your body and your body image can be understood, managed, and transformed. And you can choose to cultivate more positive and life-affirming beliefs that can alter the perception—literally change—what you see when you look into your mirror.

Explore your body image, perception, and emotions with this mindfulness practice.

1. Take a comfortable position and breathe mindfully for a few moments. When you are ready, hold one of your hands in front of you and look at it. Look mindfully, noticing the shape of your fingers, the lines, the spaces between the fingers, any color tones, and other features. Just look. When you notice thoughts, let them be, and return attention to directly observing—really seeing—your hand. Notice any sensations. Know the sensations of tingling or warmth, for example, or the sensation of heaviness or pulses. When your mind wanders, gently come back to the sensations. Notice how what we call a "hand" is, moment by moment, made up of different components—appearance, sensations, the thought that forms and creates the name "hand"—and how we can have more

thoughts about the different components ("I don't like how my fingers look," for example) that are not the same as the appearance or the sensations.

2. Practice this same way with other parts of your body or with your whole body—bringing mindful attention and focusing upon a region or body part, seeing it, knowing the sensations flowing there and noticing the thoughts or moods that arise in your mind. What do you notice when you are being mindful of your body and your inner thoughts and feelings? Are the thoughts you notice about your body really true?

Remember, there is no right or wrong, and you cannot make a mistake. This practice is an exploration of what it means to live in your body as well as a path of discovery to reveal your deeply held ideas, judgments, and attitudes that operate and impact your well-being in literally every moment.

End the Race with Anger

You're going along with your perfectly normal day, following your regular routine, when suddenly your anger comes to life—like a racehorse, agitated, with nostrils flaring. And like that horse, your anger takes off—you can't stop it or control it. Your body races, too: your heart rate quickens, your breathing becomes short and erratic, and your muscles tense up. There's no end in sight, no finishing line, just you and your anger racing along at top speed, pounding along the racetrack—your body pulsating with tension and adrenaline.

Thankfully, there is a way to exit from the race with anger. It's called mindfulness. Mindfulness-based practice can help you to pause long enough to make different choices about whether you want to keep running or to stop and take a breather, whether you want to escalate or de-escalate your anger. This next practice develops awareness and clarity about what you are experiencing, and offers an immediate choice about continuing or stepping back from the raging storm of anger that has come into the present moment. Take this moment to explore a mindful practice to help you restore your body to a place of quiet calm and relaxation, a place where choice about your next move or next moment lives and thrives.

1. Find a comfortable and safe place to sit or stand, and start by connecting to your breath. Remember each breath is your guidepost for being here in the present. Take this time to feel each breath—notice how you are breathing, what the air feels like in your nose and mouth, the pace of your breath, and the gap between your in-breath and your next out-breath.

2. Now, pay close attention to the sensations in your body where you store your anger and where your anger tends to hold your body hostage. Notice what's going on with your heart rate. Can you feel your pulse in your skin, your temples, or your fingertips? Where do you notice tension in your body? You don't need to change anything. Simply notice what you feel in your body when anger arises and be with those feelings in your body.

3. Next, allow and acknowledge—without judging—whatever thoughts or feelings come up. Take this time to just step back and watch your anger and tension, and let it be just as it is. It is neither right nor wrong, neither good nor bad. Allow yourself to be an observer at the racetrack: each horse is some maddening thought, feeling, or sensation, moving around the track at lightning speed. You are an outsider who is taking in the race, the horses, the emotions, and the day. You are a gentle witness but not a participant.

4. At times, you may notice that you get distracted by unrelated thoughts about something from your past or some new worry about the future. If you find yourself drawn away from the present moment, your feelings of anger might intensify. When this occurs, return to your breath and nudge yourself into the now—you'll notice your anger loosen and settle down. Return to exactly where you are now. Observe the colors in the room, notice the feel of the floor beneath your feet, or feel the heat in your hands.

5. Say aloud or to yourself, *I am staying in this present moment. There is nowhere else that I need to be more than right here. My thoughts live inside my mind. My mind lives inside my body. My body is doing just what it needs to do.*

During this mindful pause, you free up your mind and body to make different choices about your reaction to anger. When you pause and reconnect with your breath, you provide an opening to be an observer instead of a reactor, a witness instead of a racer rushing to the finish line.

3.

Peaceful Body, Peaceful Sleep

Have you ever been so angry that you couldn't sleep? Your anger racks your body with agonizing thoughts, feelings, and bodily sensations. You find yourself so invested in seething and keeping your anger alive that insomnia sets in. Anger is a lousy bed partner; it can sabotage a night of sleep. You need your rest in order to have the strength to fulfill your enormous responsibilities, but you can't seem to unwind from your embittered feelings. What do you do when anger won't let you get a good night's sleep?

The following mindful practice will help you find the peace and calm that you desperately need to make it through night, get the rest that you require, and feel refreshed and revived by morning. It will also help you to stop and simply notice what is here. You can do this meditation sitting upright or lying down, whichever feels more comfortable.

1. Take this moment to pause and commend yourself for committing to this practice of being in the now, despite how long and hard you've been wrestling with your anger. You are consciously making a decision to invite mindfulness into your mind and your body in order to foster peace of mind and relaxation of body.

2. Connect with your breath. Notice every minute detail of your breathing—the rise and fall of your chest, the warm air and the cool air, the air filling your lungs and leaving again, the sound of the air being drawn in and being let go.

3. Now, observe any thoughts, feelings, or physical sensations that occur at this time. You may notice that you have a cramp in your shoulder or your feet ache from being on them all day. You may notice that you're still holding on to some resentment toward your spouse, a friend, or some stranger who nearly ran you off the road the other day. You may be thinking about what you wish you had said to that insensitive salesclerk who charged you incorrectly. Be aware of the variety and scope of whatever comes to mind.

4. As you notice different thoughts and experiences, just acknowledge them with compassion. You might say, "Oh, there's my anger returning about something that happened years ago" or "There's my anger returning to that incident yesterday." Without judging yourself as a good person or a bad person, simply let yourself experience whatever it is that comes up. Without clinging to or resisting what comes to mind at this time, simply allow yourself to witness any thoughts and

feelings as they arise. You may start to notice that your thoughts and sensations keep changing—some are intense, some are mundane, some are frustrating, some are illogical, some are infuriating, some are just plain silly. Notice how they change and fluctuate, rise and fall away, come and go again.

5. If you start to feel yourself drift off, that's okay. Let your attention come back to your anger, and keep watching. You don't have to fight the anger. Anger eventually tires out and yearns to be cradled in compassion and tenderness. Take this moment to be with your breath, and allow yourself to be truly tender with your body. Each breath is a bridge to being present again. All there is, is this moment now.

May sleep embrace you and wrap you delicately in her arms like a newborn baby held in a mother's arms under a star-filled sky.

Be Kinder to Your Anger

Upset and anger can come quickly when you see someone taking advantage of another or if your property is damaged or stolen, or when you feel someone is humiliating you in public. Rude, disrespectful, or harmful behavior may come in the form of small or large irritation. Either way, it can fester, leaving you feeling affronted, provoked, and infuriated. You may want to scream at someone, throw a heavy object at the wall, or take some other kind of action in order to release your anger. When you feel outraged, disregarded, and ready to explode, you may clench your fists or teeth, and you may feel an irresistible urge to direct your anger at someone or something. Where should you go from here?

The good news is that mindfulness and compassion are your allies when anger takes hold and you feel like lashing out. The next mindfulness-based practice will help you to cultivate more tenderness and warmheartedness for your mind and body, even in the throes of upset. Let's try it now.

I. Start with the breath. Each breath that you notice and observe is a confirmation and affirmation that you are alive right now in this moment. Each in-breath is an opportunity to pay attention to your mind and body. Each out-breath is an opening for growth and change in your perspective. Be here now, with your breath, for several minutes.

2. Take this moment to notice what agitates you or ruffles your feathers. You may be experiencing extreme frustration and resentment. Many things can occur in your day that feed your anger. Just notice what thoughts and sensations arise without trying to change or fix them. Simply let them be.

3. Now, pay attention to what is good about right now. Perhaps you've had a nice meal and feel sated and full. Perhaps your car is running smoothly. Perhaps you feel particularly good in your outfit. Perhaps you've completed an important work project and there's a sense of accomplishment and relief. Take a mindful moment to breath in the goodness and exhale what you perceive to be wrong.

4. Now, consider the times when you were guided by the power of tenderness and compassion from within. Perhaps it was when your child spilled his drink everywhere and you didn't let it upset you. Perhaps it was a time when you let someone go ahead of you in line because you weren't in a hurry and it felt good to be kind to a stranger. With each in-breath and out-breath, take in those occasions or memories of being kind and know that they reside in you and are always a part of who you are.

When you take the time to be with what is—the suffering of anger and resentment and feeling wronged—you'll come to find that these difficult times will drain out of you. In the "now," you have the power to pause and develop kindness and empathy for yourself and others. It won't be easy or simple to reconnect with your tenderness and understanding. It takes time and practice, so don't berate yourself if compassion doesn't spring into action after one try. Compassion is cultivated one breath at a time, until eventually each breath infuses your next move or thought with more kindness, tolerance, and understanding as well as a willingness to accept what is and simply let it be without lashing out.

5.

Befriend Your Angry Body, Anxious Mind

For many people, anger and anxiety go hand in hand. Recent studies have shown that anger intensifies and exacerbates the symptoms of anxiety. In fact, irritability, often experienced with anger, is also a symptom of generalized anxiety disorder. For example, it can start when you listen to the morning news. The sheer injustices and horrors in your world are enough to darken your outlook and increase your anxiety. You feel worried that the world is in grave danger, literally spiraling out of control, and angered by a sense of powerlessness. In fact, the more angry you get, the more anxious, fearful, and worried you may become. These feelings may show up in your body in physical ways, such as feeling shaky, unsettled, restless, and extremely tense. What can you do? Where should you start?

This is your opportunity to befriend your angry body and anxious mind by using self-compassion. This compassion practice will help you to be kindhearted toward yourself during times of unease and discomfort.

1. Feel free to sit or stand in a comfortable position.

2. Begin by reflecting on what is bothering you. You might feel the urge to resist or ignore your fears, upset, or displeasures. What causes your anxiety in this moment? Are you worried about something from the past or the future? Are you concerned about a big decision that's weighing heavily on your shoulders at this time? Are you worried how you're going to get through your day when your body feels overly sensitive and agitated? Take this time to check in with your thoughts, feelings, and sensations. Try to get to the source of what's triggering your anger and anxiety and causing them to take over.

3. If you start to experience doubt about this practice working, simply notice your doubt. You may find yourself thinking, *It won't work. Nothing ever helps. I must not be doing it right. I'm never going to feel less angry and less anxious about my life.* It's okay when this happens. Simply notice it. Become aware that self-doubt has entered your mind and you can begin to deal with it. Doubt has a way of walking in and then walking out. You can acknowledge this right now. Try acknowledging the flow of your varying thoughts and feelings by saying, "Hello, doubt. Good-bye, doubt. Hello, anger and anxiety. Good-bye, anger and anxiety." These are just passing states of mind, coming and going, taking up space one minute and then exiting the next.

4. Now, ask yourself this: *What would it look like for me to offer tenderness and kindness toward myself right now? What kind of reassurance and understanding would I be willing to give myself to help ease my suffering? How can I be more compassionate and caring to myself in this moment and throughout my day?* Sit with these questions and reflect on the answers that you come up with. Perhaps you'd be willing to take a breath, be still with whatever is, and not act out anything. Perhaps you'd be willing to give yourself a hug or go for a walk or speak kindly to yourself. Perhaps you'd be willing to befriend your anger and your anxiety like a wounded child needing reassurance, sympathy, and mercy. Try it now.

6.

Free Yourself from Grudges

We've all found ourselves holding on to a grudge toward another person at some point in life. Maybe you were neglected by a parent or abandoned as a child. Maybe a sibling failed to show up for you at a time when you needed emotional support. You may have accumulated a laundry list of ways that people have wronged you, which has left you feeling angry over the years.

If you hold on to those grudges long enough, you will find that they start to show up in your body and may affect your health. We once worked with a woman whose emotional grudges flared up in her belly. If she dwelled on her grudges for too long, she would experience severe abdominal pains and digestion problems. We sent her home with a simple loving-kindness meditation to do before each meal, which proved to be helpful emotionally and physically.

Metta, or loving-kindness, is an ancient practice of connecting with the suffering of yourself as well as all beings in the world, and offering them compassion and wishing them well. When you create space to wish yourself and all beings loving-kindness from your heart, you learn to embrace life's tragedies, hurt, and grudges with more tenderness, openness, compassion, and sensitivity—both for yourself and for others. Let's do this now.

1. Start by finding a comfy seat. If you prefer, you can stand or lie down, so long as you remain attentive and alert. Bring your attention to your breath, and breathe mindfully for a few minutes.

2. Now, bring your focus to the emotions that are stirring in your heart. Pay close attention to the feelings and physical sensations that are occurring in your heart space in this moment. Without resisting, let them flow freely and warmly accept whatever arises or comes forth. You may experience some sadness, fear, disappointment, discomfort, or pain. Be with them. Simply let the feelings and sensations emerge and receive them with gentle acceptance for what they are.

3. Bring your attention to yourself. Use the following loving-kindness phrase to speak to the parts of you that feel hurt, injured, fearful, and upset. Say aloud or to yourself, *May I be showered in contentment. May I be showered in safety. May I be showered with good health. May I be showered in peace.* Remember to speak to yourself with warmth, gentleness, and kindness, wishing yourself well.

4. Reconnect with your breath, and on your next in-breath, imagine your entire body is being bathed in a healing light of loving-kindness. Do this for several breaths.

5. Next, bring to mind someone you love, perhaps a friend or family member. You are going to speak to the parts of that person's heart that feel hurt, injured, fearful, and upset. Remember to speak to this person with warmth, tenderness, understanding, and kindness, wishing wellness to him or her. Say aloud or to yourself, *May you be showered in contentment. May you be showered in safety. May you be showered in good health. May you be showered in peace.*

6. Return to your breath again, and on your next out-breath, imagine this person being bathed in a soothing, healing light of loving-kindness throughout his or her entire body. Do this for several breaths.

When you greet yourself and others with tenderness and nonjudgment, you transform your experience with grudges and painful emotions. You open yourself to a new way of moving in the world with a gentler heart and a softer and kinder perspective on yourself and others.

7.

Treat Your Pain with Compassion and Kindness

Have you ever been so fed up with feeling pain or the discomfort of illness—even a common cold—that you found yourself angry at your body or at some part of your body? Most people probably have. It is an easy feeling to fall into—the immediate sensations in your body are unpleasant, and anger and aversion to unpleasant feelings arise very quickly.

But does getting angry and rejecting pain and dis-ease in your body really help you feel any better? Probably not! In fact, the angry thoughts and judgments that fill your mind in those moments are more likely to act as a danger signal to your body and to activate or magnify the stress reaction. The result? Increased muscle tension, which in turn will probably make any unpleasant sensations feel even worse!

You can break free of this destructive and increasingly painful cycle of unpleasant sensations and anger toward your body. The understanding that arises from mindful and compassionate attention will help you. This meditation will show you how.

1. When you notice an unpleasant or painful sensation in your body, pause and give yourself some

time to respond mindfully. Pausing and turning mindful attention on your body for even a few moments can make all the difference between remaining in the distress caused by reacting with anger or touching the peaceful enduring center within you as a foundation for relating to the pain of your body.

2. Breathe mindfully for a few breaths, and when you feel ready, bring closer, mindful attention directly to the sensations in the region of your body that troubles you. Turn your full attention and kind curiosity to that place in your body and look deeply. Gently and kindly exploring the sensations with your attention, relax and let them reveal themselves. Imagine breathing mindfully directly into that area, becoming increasingly attentive and curious about the changing patterns of body sensations. For example, if you have back pain, can you relax, stop resisting the painful sensations, and allow the sensations to be just as they are—perhaps contracting and gripping or pulsing and burning? Can you feel the center of the painful area? Can you find the edges—where the unpleasant sensations fade and the other body sensations are felt again? As you look more deeply and mindfully at the changing sensations, notice

any thoughts and let them go. Return attention to the bodily sensations with patience and kindness. Notice any feelings of anger, aversion, or ill will in your heart and mind, and allow them; quietly name and watch those feelings, perhaps seeing how they, too, can change moment by moment.

3. If you wish, from time to time as you are breathing mindfully and watching the sensations, explore sending compassion to the body in pain, silently speaking kindly and directly to that area of your body, saying something like *May you be safe and free of pain*, *May you be healed*, or *I am so sorry you are not well. May I take care of you—my body—with compassion*.

Practice as long as you like, and without attachment to any outcome, even to making the pain better. Exploring and investigating with the power of compassionate, mindful attention, what do you notice?

8

Listen to Your Heart

When you feel overtaxed, overstressed, or burdened by life, you may find it's easy to lose your temper. The smallest irritation or irksome disappointment might set it off. You might feel compelled to yell, scream, shake your fist, kick a door, or berate someone. How does your body feel during your angry outburst? How does it feel after you lose your temper? Many people describe feeling hot, sweaty, and light-headed, with a sensation of pressure building in their body and of heat being generated and fueling their temper.

When your anger feels explosive, try this next practice for tuning in to your heart. If your heart could talk, what would it tell you? When you check in with what your heart is saying, you gain deeper understanding of and empathy for the source of your troubles. Tuning in to your heart can be an antidote to losing your temper.

1. Find a safe space to get comfortable; you can sit, stand, or lie down. Take this moment to notice any tightness held in your body and let yourself go limp. Relax your neck, shoulders, arms, legs, and torso. Notice any tension in your face and relax now.

2. Check in with your breath as a way to be in the present moment. Pay attention to each in-breath and out-breath. Notice the sensations of each breath as it rises and falls, coming in and going out of your body.

3. Now, turn your focus to your heart. What is happening with your heartbeat? Is it fast paced? Slow paced? Can you feel your pulse in other parts of your body, such as your face, throat, hands, or chest? Pay attention to the ways that your heart tries to communicate with you physically.

4. Now, imagine that your heart can speak to you. What might your heart say to you in this moment? Listen closely with tenderness. It might say, "I'm really scared. I feel overwhelmed right now. I need to be heard. I need some empathy and mercy." Imagine for this moment what your heart is telling you emotionally, and try to be a sensitive listener to the plight of your heart.

5. After you've tuned in to your heart, consider ways that you could be more gentle and soothing with your heart. Your heart has shared its deepest truths and its darkest caverns of vulnerability. What are you willing to offer your heart to show

that you care? What would it look like to be kinder and more sensitive to your heart, to reassure your heart and yourself? You might need a hug. You might go for a walk. Perhaps a few kind words of acknowledgment, such as "Dear heart, I hear your struggle and I send you deep empathy. I hear your pain and sadness and I send you love and courage."

When you carve out special time to be with your heart and to listen to what your heart needs, you can care for yourself in more ways than you ever thought possible. The practice of tuning in to your heart may counteract your next angry meltdown.

9.

Disentangle from Your Dark Mood

A great many people suffer from anger issues combined with depression. Who knows what triggers what—does anger trigger depression or does depression trigger anger? This may remain a mystery. However, it is common for people to experience a combination of dark-seated emotions, such as debilitating sadness or out-of-control, suicidal, or utterly hopeless feelings, while at the same time feeling infuriated, exasperated, and indignant. This emotionally challenging time may cause sleep difficulties, seriously diminish your sex drive, or leave you feeling thoroughly exhausted. How do you unravel from these complicated and disheartening emotions and still find peace of mind and harmony within your body?

Let's try a mindfulness practice that will help you more fully inhabit your body and the present moment just as it is—without needing to fix it, reject it, or push it away. When you cultivate a practice of deep embodiment and awareness of what is, you open the door of opportunity to experience the entirety of your life—your body, your thoughts, your moods—as ever-changing and transforming, impermanent and evolving. You become more than your anger, more than your depressed feelings. This meditation is about pausing and noticing what is happening right now for you.

1. Wherever you are, whatever you're doing right now, notice what is happening in your body. What sensations present themselves to you? You may be walking or cooking or texting. You may be eating or talking or shopping online. Take this moment and check in with what is going on in your body.

2. Set your intentions for this practice: "May this practice help me to untangle from my painful emotions. May this practice give me permission to acknowledge and accept any thoughts and feelings without acting on them."

3. Investigate mindfully what your body is experiencing. How is your energy level? Do you feel any aches or pains? What do you notice about your hands and feet, neck and arms, belly and back? With purposeful awareness, for at least a few in-breaths and few out-breaths, simply pay close attention to what you experience—without the need to move or act on the sensations.

4. Now, take this moment to acknowledge what is okay or satisfactory in your life. Try listing three or four things, however small. You might acknowledge that your child is safe, or you have a nice home, or you are fed and healthy. You may say aloud or to yourself, *I am not in danger at this time. I am okay.* Sit with what is stable and okay in your life and notice how it feels.

5. If your mind starts to wander off, simply return to the breath. You might feel a burning desire to check the time, answer the phone, send a text, or check your email. That's okay. Take notice of how attention gets derailed by thoughts and wanders off with them. Breathe mindfully and be aware of each breath as your body naturally brings air in and lets air out, over and over again, all on its own. Remember to stay connected with each breath.

There is tremendous power in tuning in to your body mindfully in order to fully inhabit whatever you are doing or experiencing. During times of immense sadness and suffering, allow yourself to connect with the sensations and emotions in your body. This will help you to untangle from those intense, overwhelming feelings and the need to react.

CHAPTER 4

Calming Your Angry Mind in Relationships

A woman in a mindfulness class reported that her relationship with her teenage son had improved since she began practicing mindfulness. "Before mindfulness," she said, "as soon as he talked about any problem, I would often get a little upset, sometimes angry, and would go into fix-it mode, and start telling him what to do. He would turn me off immediately, and we would both be frustrated and mad. But now that I know about mindfulness, when he comes to me with a problem, I just breathe mindfully, listening to him and to myself, without trying to fix or judge anything. I just breathe and listen. We both feel better, and sometimes after he tells me what is happening, he actually asks me what I think he should do! We can laugh about how things have changed between us!"

Bringing awareness to the changing contents of our inner lives immediately gives us more choices about how we can respond. For this woman, discovering her capacity to know her own inner reactions, and recognizing her impulse to "fix" her son's problem—without acting upon it—enabled a radical and positive shift in their relationship. This change for the better began with her increased attention and expanded awareness of the complex experience of her inner world.

Imagine a kaleidoscope, spinning and changing with colors, shapes, and patterns, each continuously emerging, connecting with its companions, and disappearing as it flows into the next emergence and expression. That process—emergence, expression, disappearance—could describe each of us as well as our personal, subjective, and ever-changing experience of life in each and every moment.

Anger and related feelings of ill will, aversion, fear, and pain often appear in our lives like the colors, shapes, and patterns in the kaleidoscope. When those emotions come, they can reflect deeper levels of hurt and fear—hurt and fear born from the memory of painful life experiences. As the energies of anger, hurt, and fear appear and form their patterns in this moment, they can feed feelings of separation and isolation. These in turn may burn brightly into the kaleidoscope of subjective experience in this moment, coloring and becoming the momentary pattern that drives how we relate to ourselves, others, and the world around us.

When we probe our experience of emotions like anger more deeply and attend to them mindfully and compassionately, we can see for ourselves some important truths about emotions. Seeing these truths—that is, becoming wiser about them—helps us to avoid or correct the distortions caused by anger and similar strong emotions and, as a result, to enjoy more satisfying relationships.

The first truth apparent from mindful attention is that any emotion we experience changes—it is not fixed or static. That emotion is not our permanent identity, even during an intense or difficult moment of a relationship. A feeling of anger changes quickly to one of fear or regret, which soon changes again into something else. Our ideas about anger may not change easily, but life is constantly changing, and so are our emotions!

Besides not being a permanent condition or a personal identity, emotions like anger do not appear out of nowhere. They arise from and depend upon particular causes and conditions. And those causes and conditions are not anger. For example, you may have noticed that you are more likely to respond with anger or irritation toward someone if you are tired or hungry. If you weren't so tired or so hungry, chances are you would not feel so angry when that person speaks to you or asks you for something.

Let's return to the image of the kaleidoscope. Imagine two kaleidoscopes side by side; as each one spins and changes within itself, they also move together, touch, and partially overlap with each other. Together they form a new, interacting expression of changing patterns that is at once unique, larger, deeper, and more multidimensional, and yet this new expression also contains the ongoing, flowing patterns contained in each individual kaleidoscope. That could describe—not perfectly, of course—the experience of being in a relationship. In the present moment—in every moment—there is always a series of changing conditions within and between each person in the relationship.

Just like the emotions changing in each of us, you might say that any "relationship" is not one single, fixed thing over time, but rather it is actually a series of changing "relationship moments" that flow through life. The complexity that is you repeatedly comes together with and separates from the changing complexity of the other person, creating new patterns of experience and interaction, which constantly appear and disappear in the present moment.

As an example, consider the momentary expression of life observable in a loving mother as she cradles her baby in her arms. Looking at the parent, one can imagine her personal kaleidoscope of changing feelings, thoughts, sensations, memories, hopes, and other elements coming together uniquely just for an instant when she holds and gazes upon her child. At the same time, the child—also a spinning kaleidoscope of changing conditions—looks back and smiles at his parent. As the baby and the parent smile at each other in that shared moment, something unique and new comes into being.

But the shared moment is temporary. It lasts only as long as parent and child smile at each other, and that particular expression of smiling with love at each other is totally dependent upon the pair of them interacting with affection and ease. In the next moment, if the child erupts into crying, the moment shifts—the inner life of the parent shifts with the shifting inner life of the child, and the unfolding of their relationship moves to another array of changing conditions.

In that moment of contact with one another, we immediately become part of a newly arising pattern that is bigger than ourselves. We always have some choice about what we add to the newly emerging pattern and how we relate and contribute to it in each succeeding moment of interaction with the other person. That applies, of course, to our relationships with any person, friend and foe alike. And, when you think about it, who and what are you *not* in relationship with? For example, there is the air you breathe and the food you eat—both of which you need to live; there are the animals, insects, and other living things, including plants, that come into your life in countless moments every day. Our lives are constantly flowing, changing, and touching other streams of life, if only for an instant or a single breath.

Mindfulness, kindness, and compassion practices can be an enormous aid in relationships because they help us to know more accurately and with more compassion what conditions are present in us and in the other person. With the clarity of mindfulness, we can choose a more skillful response, one consistent with our deepest values and intentions, in any relationship moment.

The practices in this chapter can help you explore and look more deeply—with awareness, compassion, and wisdom—at the enormous complexity of living in relationships. They can also help you to discover ways to find joy and manage the difficulties inevitable for each of us living, intertwined as we are, in complex networks of connectedness. And don't worry if you still feel anger and fear or hurt and despair in any relationship moment. When that happens, you have not failed or done anything wrong. After all, we all are only human, and being human means we will feel emotions! Our great gift as human beings is that—in any moment—we can have the experience of feeling emotion, and we have the possibility of knowing what we are feeling and of responding to what we are feeling with intelligence and compassion.

Over the next few pages, you will find nine relationship-focused mindfulness practices to use in daily life. Choose any that call to you.

Know Your Triggers

A crucial part of drawing on compassion and understanding when your anger boils over is being able to identify what triggers your anger. What sets you off? You may have had a peevish conversation with your spouse about your different parenting styles, and it has left you feeling frustrated and irritable. Maybe the conversation got cut short and you didn't have time to express all of your feelings and needs. Maybe you don't feel validated or reassured by how the conversation ended, and you're furious that your spouse didn't listen to you with compassion.

Anger shows up like an uninvited guest and demands your attention. So let's offer that uninvited guest some compassionate attention. If you take the time to determine what triggers your anger, you'll create the space you need to offer yourself the deeper compassion that you deserve in order to restore inner peace and calm. The following practice is a helpful tool to understand the triggers that lead to your anger. It will also help you know how to offer compassion to yourself in order to feel less swept up in your anger. .

1. In a comfortable and relaxed position—seated, standing, or lying down—take this moment to

pause and recognize when your anger or some other strong emotion is present. You are simply inquiring into what thoughts and feelings are bubbling up for you right now and taking notice of them. Ask yourself: *What am I feeling? What is upsetting me? What triggered my upset?* Whatever feelings arise or thoughts come up—blame, fear, discouragement, disgruntlement, desire to lash out—simply recognize them without acting on them.

2. Now, invite your anger into the room. Imagine offering your anger a comfy chaise longue to rest upon. Ask your anger these questions: "What are your triggers?" "Why do you get so upset?" "What makes you lash out?" Notice how your anger responds. Perhaps your anger tells you that it's tired of being ignored and discounted. Maybe your anger is angry about being treated disrespectfully. Maybe your anger is upset that no one ever listens, no one ever cares, no ever shows concern about anger's worries and concerns about the future. Let your anger describe every last detail of what's troubling its heart right now. You don't have fix anything. Simply try to listen to your anger the way you would like to be listened to. Try to listen to your anger with a kind and open heart.

3. Mindfully be aware of your breathing. Your breath is an opportunity to be fully present with whatever is happening for you. There's nothing more perfect nor more beautiful than this in-breath and out-breath. Each breath brings you closer to now.

4. As you return to your anger seated on the chaise longue, imagine what you would say to your anger as an offering of kindness. You might say, "Dear anger, I hear your pain and suffering. I am sending you comforting words of love and understanding. I am sending you the tenderness and loving-kindness that you need right now. May you find serenity and contentment with every breath."

What are the ways that you could provide generosity of heart and gentle reassurance to your anger? How does it feel when you speak softly and compassionately to yourself? You may discover that it's more difficult for your anger to stay on its track when you offer soothing words of tenderness.

2.

De-escalate Your Anger

Anger tends to spiral out of control. If you add another person into the mix, anger can escalate swiftly and without warning. What might start out as a minor irritation with a roommate, your teenager or other loved one, or a coworker can turn into a screaming match where sinister words are exchanged in the heat of the moment. You may capture a fleeting sane thought during an argument, such as *I should really stop yelling and calm down. This is pointless and getting out of control. I wish I could shift gears and end this battle right now.* You may feel deepening regret for any harmful and hurtful things that you said. In the heat of a disagreement filled with loud, toxic voices, it is extremely challenging to just walk away.

What if you could de-escalate your anger at will? What if we told you that mindfulness is a powerful tool for putting a monkey wrench into the grinding gears of anger? The following practice will teach you how to de-escalate strong emotions in order to return to a place of benevolence and equanimity.

I. At the moment you first notice that your conversation has taken an angry turn, give yourself permission to stop and take a mindful break. This is a critical step in de-escalation. There's nothing written in the law books that requires you to stay in an angry dispute. Problems in life are rarely resolved with clarity and kindness when two people are stressed out and talking harshly back and forth. Give yourself license right now to walk away; or, if you're feeling brave, invite the other person to take a silent break with you and share in this mindful practice.

2. During your mindful pause, follow your breath. Pay close attention to each in-breath and each out-breath. Take special notice of the feel of cool air passing into your nose, filling your lungs, expanding your chest and belly. Then notice the feel of warm air flowing out through your body, chest, mouth, tongue, and lips. Do this for several breaths.

3. Set your intentions for this practice: "May each breath bring me peace and patience with myself and others. May each breath teach me to be kind and gentle with myself and others. May each breath restore my calmness and clarity with myself and others."

4. Now, on your next in-breath, speak the word "peace" and on your next out-breath, speak the word "patience." Do this for several breaths.

5. Again, on your next in-breath, speak the word "kind" and on your next out-breath, speak the word "gentle." Do this for several breaths.

6. And again, on your next in-breath, speak the word "calmness" and on your next out-breath, speak the word "clarity." Do this for several breaths.

7. Open your awareness to all thoughts and sensations in your mind and body. Have the force and energy of anger shifted? What is happening for you now?

Remember to return to these words throughout your day and repeat them in conjunction with your breath whenever uncomfortable emotions arise.

3.

You Are Not Your Anger

We hear parents frequently complain about aggravating mornings spent hollering at their kids to get ready for school. You're juggling a million critical details for everyone's day to run smoothly—lunches, snacks, homework assignments, gym clothes, jackets, art projects, permission slips, change for the meter, water bottles, and so on. Amid the chaos, one child is having a meltdown because she can't find her favorite shoes, and another child is screaming frantically for you to come help him with his hair. During those stressful times, you may have barked to your child, "Pick out some shoes right now, or you can just go barefoot to school!" Later, you may feel ashamed and regretful about what you said, and yet you may still find yourself wound up and spewing angry words in the chaos the next morning. Several single parents have confided that they feel terrible guilt and shame after they speak in anger or in an overly scolding tone to their kids when under stress.

But stress and pressure-filled time constraints can make anyone lash out and speak unkindly, not just parents. So what can you do when the pressure is too much and you desperately want to avoid unleashing your anger verbally?

Even in the throes of anger, there is a window of opportunity for mindfulness. The next meditation is for cultivating wisdom and understanding beyond your angry mind so that you understand that anger—along with shame and regret—is a temporary condition and not who you are. Let's try it now.

1. Tune in mindfully to your breath. You may notice that you are holding your breath, or taking quick, shallow breaths, or straining to breathe. Simply notice how you're breathing and give yourself this moment to breathe freely. Each breath connects you more fully to this present moment and to how precious it truly is. Breathe mindfully for several breaths.

2. Now, what do you notice about your anger? Say your angry thoughts and feelings were like leaves blowing past. How would you describe your anger right now? At first, you may notice that you're surrounded on all sides with intensely angry thoughts, each one vying for importance. After a brief pause, you may notice how anger changes and is suddenly replaced by worrisome thoughts, then shifts back to a few angry ones, then those thoughts scatter and are followed closely by some mundane and trivial ones. If you watch your thoughts and feelings long enough, they are constantly in a state of coming and going, appearing and vanishing, demanding your attention and then dissolving into a faded memory. Simply notice the evolution of these thoughts and feelings.

3. As you come to understand that your anger is impermanent and not a fixed state of mind, you will also find that anger is not a fixed personality trait or character flaw. You are not your anger. You are merely an observer of your anger. You are watching the passing of emotional leaves. Anger, like any strong emotion, is simply part of a continuum of other nonangry states of mind—leaves passing through, being blown along with the changing current of the wind. Simply observe how thoughts and feelings of all kinds and all variations tumble along, in and out of your awareness.

4. Take this moment to say aloud or to yourself, *My anger will pass. My anger is not permanent. My anger is not who I am.*

Remember these phrases during times when your anger swells. They will help you to reconnect with the wisdom behind anger and deepen your understanding of what anger has to teach you.

4.

How to Enrich Each Moment of Any Relationship

Faith and wisdom teachers often point to the importance of acknowledging our human mortality. "Keep your death as an adviser," counsels a sage. A gravestone marker admonishes "as you are now, so once was I…as I am now so you shall be." And, no matter what each of us may think or hope for, the actual time and circumstances of our deaths are not known to us.

So, what does that mean for us and for our relationships, and possibly for any anger we feel in those relationships? Can we use the truth of our own mortality—and the mortality of others—to focus and enrich each moment of a relationship? Perhaps the most important step in reflecting on death and mortality is realizing it is important to do so. Then we can turn toward this truth in our lives, and our reactions to it, with curiosity and compassion, seeking to understand our own feelings and fears.

With mindfulness, we can look deeper at our feelings and ideas about death. How much and how often does fear of death lurk beneath the surface of our angry feelings? We may fear the loss of something, like the love of another or something we cherish. Or we may fear how we, or a loved one, might depart this life—in pain, alone, or neglected.

At first, such reflection can be difficult. But if we stick to it, returning mindfully in each moment with compassion and the intention to better understand and include all of our experience with each breath, we may begin to notice—over time and after many reflections—how our own feelings and perspectives about death shift.

Recognizing the fleeting preciousness of each moment more deeply, we can enjoy the resultant flowering of greater feelings of appreciation and gratitude. Warmed by this perspective, we may notice positive effects in how we value life, moment by moment, in ourselves and others in our relationships. With sensitive, gentle attention to our own fears and beliefs, we not only can better understand our grief when others die, but we can also find ease in accepting the reality of our own death, the inevitable moment when the in-breath does not return to our body.

Let this mindfulness practice help you investigate—with awareness, compassion, and understanding—your own questions about and reactions to death. Use the power of this reflection and what you learn through it to enrich and support all of your relationships.

1. Intentionally pause and take some time to investigate your ideas, thoughts, feelings, and fears about death—especially your own death. Begin by sitting comfortably and gathering attention in your body. Practice breathing mindfully for a time, allowing your body to relax and your mind

to settle. When you feel ready, ask yourself any question you choose related to death and dying. Here are some examples: "What scares me the most?" "How would I like my death to be?" "How do I think my death actually will be?" If you like, pause and record your responses by writing them down briefly. Stop from time to time to take a mindful breath as you record your responses.

2. Bring to mind a person you are in a relationship with. Reflect on the fact that he or she, too, is subject to death. How does this person live with that truth? How do you? Breathe mindfully, include and acknowledge all of your responses kindly and without judgment.

3. Having reflected more deeply on your own feelings and fears, at different moments—especially difficult ones—during your relationship, quietly pause and remind yourself that both you and the person with you are subject to death. As you reflect in this way, breathe mindfully and allow yourself to notice what happens in your own mind and heart. Let any understanding or compassion you feel support you in the relationship.

Stop Anger from Leaking into Your Relationships

When you're upset over a fouled-up day or a stressful occurrence that has left you feeling unsafe or uncertain, your feelings can affect everyone around you—family members, roommates, friends, and others. In fact, it may feel virtually impossible to hide your anger. Anger has a way of entering a space, taking over the whole room, and then making negative, snide remarks to innocent bystanders. You might offer a mean, sarcastic response to your partner when you're distressed by your anger. You might cut a friend off in a conversation because your anger has left you feeling perturbed and impatient. You don't mean to be mean, but it happens because anger gets the best of everyone; you might act out in inconsiderate or thoughtless ways towards the ones you care about the most.

It doesn't have to be this way. You can break this cycle of anger leaking into your relationships. Let's try the following compassion meditation to help you cultivate kindness and generosity of heart toward yourself and others in order to keep anger from overflowing into your relationships.

1. Take this moment to move away from distractions—cell phone, computer, book, laundry, and

so on—and give yourself this time to move into a deeper awareness. You might find it helpful to focus your attention on the sensations in your body or on your breath. Rest your attention there for a few minutes or for several mindful breaths. Notice what sensations come up for you. Notice how the sensations are always changing. Your ears feel hot, and then the sensation passes. Your nose itches, and then it stops. You feel stiffness in your joints, and then you notice a subtle ache somewhere completely different.

2. When you notice your anger return and accelerate, focus on the part of your body that calls for your attention. For example, when angry feelings arise, notice any tightness in your body, and then focus your awareness on the area of your body that is tense. When you think about blaming someone or lashing out, focus your awareness on the part of your body where you feel these dark and painful thoughts. When you feel hurt or scared or angry, focus your awareness on the area of your body where you feel these troubling emotions.

3. Remember to let your thoughts, feelings, and sensations be just as they are, without resisting or changing them. Everything is just as it is supposed to be.

4. Now, offer yourself goodwill and kindness. You might say aloud, "With each breath, may I find the strength to be kind and gentle with myself." Feel free to create a phrase for yourself that conveys your ability to nurture self-compassion. Repeat the phrase during these times of painful and uncomfortable emotions and be aware of what arises in you and your body.

5. Next, offer goodwill and kindness to others. You might say aloud, "May kind and gentle blessings greet you each day." Feel free to create a phrase that resonates with you and conveys the compassion that you wish for others. Notice what comes up for you and what might be shifting in your experience around anger. Make your intention for this meditation; may it deepen your awareness, and help you offer tenderness and maintain a kind and soft heart to yourself and others.

Mindful Inquiry for Relief from Anger

Relationships are complex and can stir up troubling emotions. Some of the most challenging relationships include parenting a teen, coping with an aging parent, or managing an unpleasant coworker. The constant stress and strain in your daily interactions with this person can further exacerbate your anger and leave you questioning your sanity. It's nobody's fault, but it may bring out the worst in everyone involved.

The next time communication breaks down with someone you care about or work with, leaving you feeling overwhelmed, furious, and resentful, take this time to be mindful and check in with your emotions. A mindful inquiry meditation is an invitation to bring nonjudgmental awareness into any stressful or angry interaction in order to foster more understanding of it and freedom from it.

1. Wherever you are or whatever you're doing, tune into your breathing. Notice each in-breath and each out-breath. Focus your attention on the air flowing in and out, filling and releasing, entering and exiting your body. Do this for several breaths.

2. In this moment of pausing and slowing down, recognize any thoughts and feelings that present

themselves to you. For example, you may think, *This person is really pissing me off. She's so selfish and doesn't listen to me. I could just pull my hair out with frustration.* Simply recognize the thoughts that come up for you and see them as just thoughts to make note of. What feelings are surfacing for you?

3. The next step in mindful inquiry is to acknowledge your thoughts and emotions and allow them to simply be here with you. Imagine welcoming in your thoughts and feelings right now as if they are your dearest friends. Offer them a seat in your home and treat them like treasured guests. Your feelings of anger and frustration are here with you, but they are also separate from you. Your thoughts are seated beside you, but they are also outside of you. Thoughts and feelings share the room with you, but they are only passing through on the journey through life. Remember to return to your breath in order to tap back into being present.

4. Now, take this moment to investigate where your thoughts and feelings reside in your mind and body. How does your anger feel in your mind and body? Where is the anger coming from? Where does your anger show up in your body? Simply explore how your angry thoughts and emotions affect your body, without needing to do anything or to make arrangements to change it.

5. Do not identify with your anger and do not take it personally. Remember, your thoughts and feelings are welcomed guests who will visit for awhile and then leave. Then new thoughts and feelings will arrive, stay for some time, and then leave. You feel anger now, but you are not your anger. Your anger is visiting for now but will eventually walk out the door. There is no reason to judge your thoughts and feelings as either good or bad, right or wrong. All thoughts and feelings come and go. Just notice this. How does it feel to not identify with your angry thoughts and emotions?

Mindful inquiry is an opportunity to meet and greet your intense emotions in a new way—as guests passing through—rather than with the old, familiar strategy of harshly judging yourself and others. When you shift your habits this way, you will find new sources of understanding and freedom.

7

Acting Without Anger at Home

Another arena where anger can cause havoc is at home. When you're struggling in your own life with the pressures of stress and feeling overwhelmed, you may find anger spilling into your home life. You try to bury your anger as best you can, but your anger eventually finds a target—typically someone you share space with. After an angry outburst, you find it uncomfortable to face that person later. You may even avoid her out of guilt, regret, or embarrassment.

What if we told you that turning away from your housemate actually makes it harder for you to find peace and equanimity? What if we told you that extending compassion and empathy toward yourself and others will bring you greater comfort and ease? Let's try this next meditation to do just that.

1. Find a place to sit with ease, and put away any devices or things that might distract you from fully engaging in this practice.

2. Place mindful attention on your breath, a specific sound, or a sensation in your body.

3. Now, shift your attention to the distressing and overwhelming feelings that you have right now. Observe the feelings that come up because of your feeling overwhelmed. Notice anything that you think contributes to your discomfort and stress. Take note of any role that you might play in perpetuating and feeding the distress. For example, you might lash out at others, which further exacerbates your stress and frustration. Or, you may find that blaming your roommate for the messy living room is the reason for your stress, even though you have been stressed about other things before you ever noticed the living room. Notice, and then let it be.

4. When you're ready, set your intentions for this practice. You might say, "May this practice allow me to see when I withhold tenderness and compassion for myself and others. May this practice help me to engage in kindheartedness and goodness toward myself and others. May this practice remind me that I am not suffering alone and to extend generosity and love to myself and to others." Feel free to make up your own goodhearted phrases and speak them softly and gently, breathing mindfully in between each phrase.

5. If you start to feel yourself wander away from the practice, stewing over events or conversations that happened weeks ago or that might occur in the future, simply return to your breath. By bringing close attention to the rhythm, pattern, sound, and feel of your breath, you will drop into the present moment quite swiftly.

6. Now, bring to mind someone you live with, and imagine speaking from your heart with nurturing reassurance. You might say, "May you experience tenderness and compassion. May you feel kindheartedness and goodness. May you be reminded that you are not suffering alone and that you are surrounded by generosity and love." Feel free to make up your own good-hearted phrases and speak them softly and gently, breathing mindfully in between each phrase.

Remember to be aware of any thoughts and feelings that come to mind. Let them in, let them be, and let them go. Let your warmhearted intentions settle into your body, into your consciousness. Let them support you with compassion. Let them support the other relationships in your life with empathy and equanimity. What do you notice about your mind and your body after this practice?

8.

Put an End to Faultfinding

Consumed by anger and regrets, it's easy to find fault in everyone else, even your neighbors. The slightest grievance or infraction is enough to fan the flames of negative emotions. Maybe you dislike it when your neighbor parks in front of your house. Maybe it aggravates you when your neighbor has an unkempt front lawn. Maybe you find it appalling how your neighbor never returns your hello or acknowledges you in any way. The list of complaints can go on and on. You may notice what you dislike about your neighbor more when you're having a bad day than a good day.

When you cling to what annoys and aggravates you, when you clutch at your list of complaints about other people, you feed your anger. When you take a moment for positive reflection, you starve your distressing emotions and start generating harmony within and with others. Let us show you how.

1. The first place to start is with your breath. A few mindful in-breaths and out-breaths will bring you closer to feeling relaxed, peaceful, and at ease. Simply watch and observe the sensations of your breath as it rises and falls, comes and goes, and as air fills you up and then empties out again.

2. Now, open your awareness to the positive qualities or conditions in your life. Contemplate, for a moment, the qualities of goodness that exist in the world. For example, you might contemplate peace, generosity, respect, tolerance, joy, love, kindness, and so on.

3. Now, pick the one positive quality that resonates the most with you right now and formulate a question around it. For example, "What gives me joy?" "How do I give love?" "What brings me peace?" Once you have your question in mind, speak it aloud, and then simply listen mindfully to your reply. Your joy list might consist of playing with your kids, taking the dog for a walk, going out to dinner, and so on. Your peace list might consist of times when you feel well-rested, calm, and contented.

4. If you start returning to your list of grievances and annoyances with your neighbor, check in mindfully with your breathing, ask your question again, and then listen patiently and with curiosity to your response.

5. Feel free to repeat your inquiry several times and notice what happens in your mind and your body. What sensations are you experiencing right now?

6. Now, take this moment to open and soften your heart by asking the same question on behalf of your neighbor or another person. For example, "What gives my neighbor joy?" "How does my neighbor give love?" "What brings my neighbor peace?" Imagine what your neighbor's response might be, without attaching a judgment or negative storyline. Listen intently to what your neighbor might feel if asked one of those questions. His joy list might consist of meeting up with friends, dancing, playing guitar, going to the gym, and so on.

This practice helps you to access your own inner wisdom. By doing this, you promote goodness and harmony for yourself and for others.

Learn to Listen Mindfully

When you are in a conversation, especially when the other person is telling you something personal and perhaps painful, do you hear her voice clearly, or are you busy with your own inner voices, lost in your own reactions to what she is saying?

Pausing to listen mindfully, giving full and nonjudging attention to what the other person is saying, can be a very illuminating and empowering experience. We may notice how much our own inner reactions take our attention away from the other person, or by attending mindfully experience more clarity in our own understanding of what she is saying and feeling.

Mindful listening is an act of great generosity, because we are giving another the gift of our wholehearted presence. Mindful listening can be challenging because it requires us to notice and care for our own distress as we hold the other in our attention. We may notice when the pain or fear of another arouses similar feelings in us, and also notice our inner desire to escape that pain. When we practice mindful listening, we can breathe quietly and remain present for our friend without speaking and changing the subject, or trying to suggest a "fix"—which is, usually, really intended to relieve us of our own painful feelings, feelings that have arisen in reaction to what they are saying! With mindful listening, we create a safe space for the other to speak, one that allows that person to hear her own inner voices more clearly as well as the experience of speaking her own truth to another person without fear, being heard and feeling the caring presence of another human being.

You can practice mindful listening—quietly hearing and allowing the other's voice and your own—in any conversation. Sensitive, nonjudging attention is all you need, along with the willingness to be still and listen. Take these simple instructions with you, and see for yourself what can happen when you listen to others and to yourself with more awareness and kindness.

1. In any conversation, or before one begins, decide and intend to be more mindful and to bring close attention to all the details of the conversation with the other person.

2. Gently rest attention on your breathing as an anchor in the present moment, and breathe mindfully for a few breaths. During the conversation, you can return to mindful breathing whenever you feel lost, disconnected, or confused.

3. During the conversation, allow yourself to relax and sit quietly, listening mindfully to your partner. Deliberately restrain yourself from

speaking or gesturing often, and simply listen quietly as the other person speaks. This may seem strange at first, but relax and trust that you have what you need.

4. Breathe mindfully, feeling your breath as you listen. As your attention settles, listen to your own inner voice as well. What is your own mind saying? What is it telling you to do or say? Is your inner voice upset? Does it wish to leave or change the subject?

5. When you choose to respond, notice how that happens. What are you feeling? Trust yourself to speak mindfully and from your heart. What do you notice when you are able to hear both voices—the other person's and yours—in your mindful conversation?

CHAPTER 5

Calming Your Angry Mind at Work

What did you do at work today?

This is such a common question. But how often do you respond "I practiced patience," or "I noticed and took care of my feeling of being stressed out," or "I developed more of my good qualities of heart working with difficult coworkers," or "I practiced being in each moment with full attention to what I was doing, did a good job—and I enjoyed myself!"?

While our work is naturally focused on achieving particular goals or outcomes, it is also true and undeniable that our functioning at work depends upon a complex and rich interaction between our inner lives and the lives and circumstances unfolding around us. For example, have you ever noticed how your interactions in and the effectiveness of your work are related to your own state of mind? When you are rested and alert or open and feeling good about things, do your work and your relationships with others go better? And how do things go when you are not feeling well, are distracted, or upset?

A person in a mindfulness class reported, with surprise in his voice, that his experience of anger at work had changed during the weeks of being in the class and practicing mindfulness. "I noticed the other day," he said, "when things got really hectic in the emergency room where I work, that I was not using profanity as much as I used to. I was just talking to people and

I felt calmer, even though things were really stressful." He went on to say, "I think my coworkers were pleasantly surprised!"

Work—whether you are being paid for your time and activity or not—is a place where you will probably spend the majority of your waking hours over your lifetime. And, interestingly, while you may have little control over the external conditions of your work life, the one place you can hope for some control is your inner life.

You can develop more control over your inner life—your thoughts and feelings about what happens to and around you at work—through greater awareness. And, as you have already learned, mindfulness helps you develop greater awareness. Instead of ignoring painful or angry feelings, becoming lost in them, or projecting or acting out your feelings onto others, with mindfulness you have a means not only for truly understanding your thoughts and feelings but also for relating to them differently. Mindfulness offers you both the source of real freedom as well as the possibility for real change.

Researchers have found that workers are much more productive and satisfied when they take regular breaks to rest and recharge at work, when they feel valued and appreciated by others for their efforts, when they are able to focus on their tasks and have some control over when and where they do them, and when they are able to do what they do best and enjoy most because they feel connected to a higher purpose or larger vision through their work.

Learning to bring mindful and compassionate attention to your body, thoughts, emotions, reactions, and relationships will help you calm your angry mind at work. But that's not all. It can also reveal a rich and fascinating world of new possibilities for rest and recharging, valuing and appreciating your work and that of others, focusing your attention, and embodying and connecting with your deepest values in each action and each moment.

Becoming more mindful at work can have a positive impact on your success, too. Research has linked mindfulness practice to increased emotional and social intelligence. These two kinds of intelligence are important because of their impact on people's sense of satisfaction and success, not only at work but also in life.

But be warned! Bringing mindfulness to each moment and each situation in your work life can also reveal the stress, the depth of challenges, the pain of strong emotions like anger and fear, and the constriction and restriction within that can come from your deeply held personal judgments and beliefs. Bringing mindfulness to work takes courage and curiosity. It also takes discipline and trust in yourself. In mindfulness-based stress reduction classes, we caution that becoming more mindful in your life usually means that it gets more stressful before it gets less stressful! This is simply because as people grow in mindfulness, they must face how much pain and stress they are actually carrying in their life, their relationships, and, of course, in their work.

As you do these practices, learning to bring mindfulness and compassion to yourself and to others in the work you do every day, you may also experience some tension as you follow the path of mindful awareness. Sometimes you may not want to pay attention or be mindful at all! Although a part of you may desperately seek the peace and ease of being truly present and working with full attention, clarity, and resilience, another part of you may wish to be left alone and undisturbed. Who hasn't felt the desire to just go in, do the job, and go home?

This tension between seeking satisfaction and deeper meaning in our actions and the desire to be undisturbed is simply part of the human condition. It is a form of the basic tension we all experience between our longing for well-being and belonging, and the accumulated pain of the burdens we carry. It is not a failure or a defect to experience this tension. It's simply more evidence that we are all human, after all!

The practices in this chapter offer you many ways to bring mindfulness into your working life. With these various practices, you can extend any of the three meditative paths we have been exploring into your work life. If you follow the first path, you could pause and notice with increasing clarity, sensitivity, and understanding when anger is present. Or, if you follow the second path, you might engage a practice focused on touching and extending kindness and compassion to cool the fires of anger. If you follow the third path, you might reflect more deeply on the nonanger elements present in a sudden burst of anger and see a way to soothe your fear and upset or to uproot a deeply held yet no longer relevant idea or belief.

So, relax and explore these mindfulness-based practices. They don't have to be just more "work!" Take your time with them. Let them become your close friends and best allies. Remember, you already have all that you need. Mindfulness, kindness, and wisdom are already there within you.

Over the next few pages, you will find nine mindfulness practices you can use in your working life. Choose any that call to you.

Really? I Don't Have to
Be a Superhero?

In the opening introductions, a woman in a mindfulness class disclosed that she took the class because she was burning out from taking care of her spouse, whose health was deteriorating because of a chronic illness.

Another person, a health care professional, said, "I am here because I am never satisfied with myself. I go home at night after seeing ninety-nine patients in the clinic and beat myself up because I didn't see a hundred."

Sound familiar? How often do we exacerbate our own stress? How often do our inner judges and critics say we have not done enough? The inner judgments and criticism can fuel anger that obscures the truth of our situation. We may tell ourselves we haven't done enough despite the fact that we're exhausted from the heavy load we already carry.

A few weeks later at the mindfulness class we mentioned above, participants shared that, by practicing mindfulness, they had learned to be more self-aware of their inner judges and critics. They had begun to recognize the stress they carried in their bodies as they did their jobs, day after day. They had also begun to ask others for help as well as to give themselves more time away from their work or caregiving for resting and recharging.

They also disclosed that they had finally come to accept and find peace in the fact that there was only so much they could actually do to ease the pain of the people they cared for. One of the most powerful meditations, they said, was the one for caregivers that taught compassion plus equanimity with simple phrases like "May I see my limitations with compassion, just as I view the suffering of others," "I wish you peace and ease, and I cannot control the course of life and death," and "May this situation teach me the true meaning of life."

Let this meditation support you in growing awareness of your own caregiving burdens, whatever they are, and in accessing self-compassion and equanimity for all that you do.

1. Take some time for yourself and for this meditation. Make yourself comfortable and begin with gathering attention mindfully in the changing sensations of your body. Simply feel the sensations, the weight of your body, the pulses, contractions, and expansions—not trying to make anything happen but relaxing and gently noticing.

2. Gently bring attention to the sensations of your breathing, and settle into mindful breathing for a time. Let yourself rest in the ease of simply noticing and allowing the sensations of your breath to flow through awareness in this moment.

    When you are ready, reflect on the sense of burden you feel with your work of caregiving. You might ask yourself questions like these: "What is so difficult for me with this work?" "How do I feel?" "What does my body experience?" "Where is the burden and the pain of this work in my body? My heart? My mind? My relationships?" Without judgment, notice any thoughts or feelings that arise. Trust yourself to remember to respond kindly and wisely to these parts of yourself.

3. Return to mindful breathing from time to time during your reflection. Let the ease and simplicity of each mindful breath remind you of your basic goodness and intelligence, and rest there.

Practice for as long as you like. If you like, at times during the meditation or at the end, wish yourself well, perhaps using a phrase like "May I see my limitations with compassion, just as I view the suffering of others" or "May this situation teach me about the true nature of life."

In with the Good, Out with the Stress and Anger

Anger and stress are synonymous for a great many people, particularly at work. Have you ever noticed the role that stress plays in your anger? If you're prone to anger in the workplace, then mounting stress, responsibilities, and deadlines can certainly exacerbate your angry behaviors.

For many, managing anger is directly linked with managing stress levels. You may find it hard to imagine that a few mindful breathing techniques can help you with your anger and your stress, but we promise that, with practice, you will move more freely and easily in both your mind and body during times of overwhelming stress and intense emotions. Let's get into the practice now.

1. Find a comfortable space to sit or stand. If you can take this practice outside into a spacious and beautiful environment, that would be ideal. You can also do this seated at your desk or work site. Wherever you are, take a brief moment to close your eyes gently and rest.

2. Upon opening your eyes, bring all your attention to your breath. Notice each breath as it comes

and goes. Notice how you're breathing—the pace, rhythm, effort, capacity, level, and so on. What does the air feel like when you inhale? What does the air feel like when you exhale? Notice every nuance and subtle aspect of your breathing in a mindful way.

3. Now, with each in-breath, whisper the word "good" and visualize a gust of air brimming with goodness and filling every part of your mind and body. Imagine the good filling every cell and every organ and flowing through your bloodstream. Let the goodness in, saturating your body with warmth, peacefulness, and ease of movement. Your mind and heart are comforted in good at all times with each breath.

4. Now, with each out-breath, whisper the words "stress and anger," and then visualize a release of all negativity from every part of your body. Imagine the stress and anger draining from every cell, every organ, and your bloodstream. Let it all out. Let the heaviness of dark emotions fall away without resisting it, or getting in the way, or clinging to it. Your mind and body have no use for the stress and anger, and can release them at any time with each breath.

5. If you start to experience anger slipping in or if nagging thoughts about your stress interrupts

your mindfulness practice, simply return to your breath and pay closer attention to what is happening around your breathing. You will naturally become more present when you tune in to your breath in a conscientious and intentional fashion.

Allow yourself to ride the waves of each in-breath and each out-breath as often as you need and as often as anger and stress arise. Remember to rely on this simple mindful breathing technique when painful emotions come up for you at work. It will help you find more peace of mind throughout your day.

3.

Let Forgiveness into Your Heart

If you work with others—at a job site, in an office building, in retail, or elsewhere—then you've probably had a run-in with your anger and a coworker. It happens. You may have felt misunderstood, mistreated, or judged harshly for something during a meeting, a conversation, or an email exchange. If it happens more than once, you may find it hard to let it go. Maybe you still ruminate on the negative interaction with that coworker. Maybe you avoid spending time with him socially at lunch or on a break. Maybe you still feel lingering anger and resentment at her, despite how much time goes by.

You can learn to loosen the clutches of anger by making a practice of forgiveness. Let's be truthful: forgiveness is challenging. You may find it very hard to imagine offering forgiveness to that coworker (or anyone else). But if you can forgive, you'll find that it is an important step toward healing and well-being for yourself and others. Keep in mind that forgiveness does not mean you are condoning or giving approval. In fact, forgiveness is largely for your own benefit, and it doesn't have to involve anyone else. The following mindfulness and compassion practice will assist you in extending forgiveness and restoring inner tranquillity and calm.

1. Find a comfortable place to sit or stand, and take several mindful breaths. When you feel more

rested, present, and connected to your breath, begin to move your attention to this meditation on forgiveness.

2. Set your intentions now. You might say, "May this practice help me to release any feelings of resentment or grudges that I carry with me day after day at work," "May this practice help me to acknowledge and heal any hurt that I may have caused to another person," "May this practice bring deeper healing, understanding, and calmness to me and to others."

3. Bring to mind someone who you have animosity toward, or have been hurt by, or whose actions raised feelings of indignation. It could be a coworker, supervisor, or client from the past or the present. The hurt could be from a minor annoyance, a negative, off-hand remark, a hostile tone of voice, or dealings with an argumentative coworker. Remember to breathe mindfully, connecting to your heart, where your well of kindness and tenderness resides. Then picture yourself offering gentle words to this person. Whisper these words lovingly, "For any ways that you have hurt me, now or in the past, consciously or unconsciously, I offer you my forgiveness. For any

ways that I have hurt you, now or in the past, consciously or unconsciously, I accept your forgiveness." Feel free to come up with your own words of forgiveness for yourself and for the other person if these don't suit.

4. Remember to extend forgiveness without expectation or attachment to the outcome. You are merely offering grace and compassion as a way to release the pain of clinging to resentment and grudges.

5. You may notice that a myriad of emotions come up during your practice. That's okay. If you start to feel sadness or fear, focus gentle awareness on what is happening in your body and practice breathing mindfully. As the feelings subside, return to extending your words of forgiveness to yourself and the other person.

The power of forgiveness is the key to keeping you on the path to feeling lighter, freer, and happier. It's a generous gift to offer to yourself and others on your personal journey toward healing and wellness.

4.

Letting Go of Aversion and Ill Will

A great deal of stress, aggravation, and sense of injustice can come from interactions with an overbearing or micromanaging boss. A minor disagreement or cutting remark can send you back to your project with a feeling of ill will and aversion. *Aversion* is a desire to turn away or avoid something, such as a person or situation, because of a strong dislike. Maybe your boss gave you an assignment without enough time to do the job as thoroughly as you'd like. Maybe your boss pointed out a small flaw in your work. Maybe you had an argument about how best to organize a project and now you feel like your ideas were dismissed too easily. Maybe you feel disrespected or taken for granted by your boss.

Endless scenarios can occur between you and your superiors, coworkers, or friends that might fuel your anger. So, what wisdom can be learned from your anger? Is there a way for you to release feelings of aversion and ill will? The next practice will teach you mindfulness skills for letting go of ill will and finding balance and equanimity.

1. Give yourself permission to take a brief meditation break. Feel free to sit or stand, as long as you

feel alert and attentive. You should be proud of yourself for carving out this time for good self-care of your mind and body.

2. Connect with your breath, paying mindful attention to the flow of air in and the flow of air out. Use your senses to help you notice specific aspects of your breathing, focusing on the sound or the physical sensation of each breath.

3. When you feel more settled and relaxed, take this moment to watch and welcome any thoughts of ill will as they come to mind. Simply allow yourself to be curious. You might be thinking, *I hate my boss. I envy his position. He's so controlling. I wish he'd get off my back. I wish I could give him a piece of my mind.* What thoughts and feelings come up for you?

4. Now, breathing mindfully, notice how the thoughts present themselves in your body. What sensations do you notice? Pay attention to the unpleasantness and the sensation of aversion that crops up in your experience for this moment. How does animosity feel in your body? Each time you notice one of your dislikes or feelings of animosity, simply name it aloud. "This is a dislike. Feelings of dislike. This is an aversion. Aversion.

Aversion." Simply name the aversion, without getting caught up in your anger or needing to alter or push away your situation. Allow yourself to remain watchful, curious, welcoming, and non-judging. What happens in your thoughts when ill will and aversion are there? What have you learned about your dislikes and aversions? What is being revealed to you from your meditation?

This exercise isn't easy or simple. Finding balance and equanimity may not happen in a five-minute meditation. It will take practice and commitment, naturally. The good news is that when you observe and name your aversions, they lose their power over you and they simply become fleeting thoughts that come and go. In time, acknowledging that your aversions are only temporary can come as a great relief and help restore your sense of balance and equanimity.

5.

Comfort Your Sorrow

Psychologists write often about the link between anger and sorrow, and how anger can be a mask for sorrow and grief. Maybe you can recall a time when you felt frustration and anger over a disturbing situation, which in turn left you utterly hopeless and depressed. If your anger greets you during morning traffic or over cold coffee and plants itself right on your desk at work or at your job site at the end of your eight-hour shift, you may then experience serious bouts of sorrow. Anger and sorrow walk a similar heavy emotional path. They both need extra care and attention.

This mindful practice will help you to bring self-compassion and tenderness to your angry mind and feelings of sorrow. You will gain skills for comforting yourself when you feel burdened with sorrow. Compassion and understanding are wise tools for self-soothing, healing, and nurturing. Let's begin now.

1. Breathing mindfully, take a moment to set your intentions for your practice. Say aloud or to yourself, *May this practice deepen my awareness of my pain and suffering. May this practice teach me to be more caring and compassionate to myself.*

2. Now, take this time to sit with your anger and sorrow. Notice what painful feelings and thoughts come up for you right now. What distresses you at the moment? Maybe you are struggling with a personal issue, such as a mental or physical health challenge. Maybe you're focused on a work-related hassle. Maybe you feel burdened with sorrow by some horrific tragedy that you heard on the news. What's coming up for you?

3. When you feel ready, invite your troubling thoughts, feelings, and sensations into the room and offer them a comfy couch. If you could offer caring words to your sorrow, what would you say? Imagine that your sorrow is like a crying baby. Look after your sorrow and make it as comfortable as you would that crying baby. Perhaps you would grab an extrasoft blanket to wrap your sorrow in. Perhaps you would soothe your sorrow with pillows, warmth, and affectionate touch.

4. When, in order to avoid your distressing emotions, your mind starts to wander, simply notice that this is happening. You might feel the urge to check the time or write a note to remind yourself about something later, or let yourself be distracted by noise from the street. Call out to yourself whatever the distraction is, name it

a distraction, and return to breathing mindfully, without acting on the impulse to get up or move or change anything. Let whatever is just be what it is.

5. What kind of tenderness and kindness would you offer your sorrow in words? Using a compassionate tone, gently whisper these words, "I feel and acknowledge your sorrow and anger, and I am sending you deep love. I feel your painful emotions, and I am sending you nurturing thoughts and reassurance. I feel your troubling feelings, and I am sending you tenderness and patience." It's okay to make up your own compassionate phrases. Continue to repeat them over and over, as many times as you like.

How does it feel in your mind and body when you send these comforting words to yourself? The more caring and tender you are with your sorrow and your anger, the more readily you'll calm down, start to heal, and feel validated.

6.

Find Your Stillness Within

If your work requires a great deal of travel, then finding a quiet place to cope with your anger can be challenging. Anger can show up when you're flying across the country, driving in a car, riding on a bus, or traveling on your bike. When you're mad and driving, you may try to push the anger further down by turning the music up. When you're angry and seated next to strangers on a bus or plane, you may fidget restlessly or play a game on your cell phone. Maybe you ruminate on your anger, letting it grow bigger and more unwieldy, until you find yourself contemplating something self-destructive, like drinking alcohol, hitting another car, or driving off a cliff.

Not everyone has the luxury of a meditation room to go to when filled with angry thoughts and emotions, but one of the simple beauties of mindfulness is that you can be mindful at any time and in any situation. Mindfulness is a skillful teacher who accompanies you on your travels wherever you go. This practice is for those times when you are traveling or you have no privacy. It will help you to find peace in the stillness of each unfolding, present moment.

I. Being mindful can start easily by being fully present with your breath. Yes, it's that simple. The more closely you pay attention to your breath, the more you are able to restore tranquillity and ease to your mind and body. So let's begin with the breath.

2. Whether you're flying on a plane, operating a vehicle, or riding in a car, take a few mindful breaths. Notice your breath—when you breathe in and when you breathe out. You might say to yourself inwardly, *I am breathing now. Each breath is keeping me alive. Breathing in now. Breathing out now. Breathe in. Breathe out.* You don't need to stop what you're doing. You can simply tune in to your breathing and notice what is happening with each breath.

3. No matter what you're doing, find the stillness in each breath. Maybe you've never noticed it before. So take this moment to pay close attention to the quiet, still moment of each in-breath and out-breath. You may notice it at the top of your in-breath, when you've brought all of your air into your lungs and then for a split second, there it is—your stillness. Or you may notice it at the bottom of your out-breath, when you've released all of your air from your lungs and for a fleeting nanosecond, there it is—your stillness. Where is your stillness? Try to connect with it now. It sits with your breath at all times, wherever you go. It lives within you and is available to you at any time.

When you connect with your breath, you connect with your constant companion, stillness. In the stillness, you will find the reassuring promise of peace and quietude. Let the stillness greet your anger and your stress. Let the stillness and the tranquillity ease into your mind and body, into your driving and parking, into your bus transfer and your taxi ride. When you befriend your breath, you naturally befriend each calm, still moment within you on your journey.

7.

Discover Your Beginner's Mind

Work is stressful enough without adding anger into the mix. Anger inhibits your concentration and ability to focus. Anger is difficult to shrug off easily and can distract you with annoying thoughts and feelings of irritability. You might find yourself feeling aggravated with a complicated spreadsheet because the numbers are still not adding up correctly. You might feel indignant over being recently passed over for a raise or promotion, and, as a result, you find it extremely difficult to focus on a single task.

This mindfulness practice will teach you how to have a beginner's mind. (See chapter 1 for more on beginner's mind.) This will help you to shift your perspective, improve your ability to concentrate, and center your attention where you need it the most: at work.

1. Find a comfortable position and, if you are willing, close your eyes and allow the muscles in your face to relax. Consciously notice any muscle tension and let it go.

2. When you feel more relaxed and settled, open your eyes and connect with your breath. Take a

few mindful in-breaths and out-breaths, loosening and slacking your body with each breath. Experience your breathing with close awareness. Notice how air feels entering into your nose or mouth. Notice how air feels exiting your nose or mouth. Don't try to modify or change your breathing. Simply notice your breath as it naturally occurs, as it naturally happens.

3. When you feel anchored in your breath, recognize any angry thoughts, feelings, or sensations that may surface for you. What's making you angry right now? How is your anger affecting your work? Where do you feel the anger in your body? Without moving or fixing it, simply notice what comes up for you. Notice the discomfort and let it just be what it is.

4. Now, imagine that you are experiencing everything as if for the first time. Your anger and your discomfort are new and fresh to you, as though you've never felt them before. What would that be like for you? A beginner's mind is like a child's mind in the sense that you're willing to be curious and filled with wonder about everything around you or happening in you. Give yourself permission to have a child's perspective. Can you be a child and explore what is happening with wonder and curiosity? Allow yourself to let go of any idea that you already know all about something.

5. With your beginner's mind, ask yourself these questions: *What is anger? What is this thought that I am having? Where did this new feeling come from?*

6. Investigate a little further. When you explore your anger as if for the first time, what happens for you? What do you notice about your anger now?

When you experience anger, you are likely preoccupied with thoughts and emotions about what's going to happen. Because you already have preconceived notions about your anger and the possible outcome, you find it hard to simply live in the present moment.

Everyone possesses a child's mind. You carry this tool or attitude of curiosity with you wherever you go. Use it as a way to relate to your anger in new ways and improve your ability to focus and concentrate on what needs to get done.

8.

Welcome Each Thought with "Yes"

Not all people love their jobs. Maybe the very thought of work is enough to make you seethe with anger and resentment. A good morning can swiftly turn gloomy when you feel stuck in your job, or you work with unpleasant people, or your work doesn't give you any pleasure. Job dissatisfaction mixed with anger is a cocktail for daily grouchiness and irritability.

Although you may not be able to find another job right this minute or transfer to a different position or department, your situation is still an opportunity for awareness and mindfulness. You can become more aware about what's going on for you in your immediate experience of anger. This awareness will enable you to shift away from angry responses and reactions to more carefully considered behaviors. This mindfulness-based practice will teach you how to explore being in the present moment as a way to calm your angry mind at work.

1. Find a place where you can be quiet, if possible, and get into a comfortable position. Feel free to sit or stand, remaining awake and alert.

2. Bring mindful attention to your breath, noticing the flow of air in and the flow of air out. In and out. Next, bring mindful attention to any

sensations in your body. You might notice your chest rising with each in-breath. You might notice the warmth of your arms resting against your sides. You might hear a little rumbling in your belly. Notice the sensations and then let them be.

3. Now, notice any anger or upset feelings that are present at this time and be mindful of them. With an open and kind heart, continue to breathe mindfully, and then acknowledge and recognize any difficult emotions. When the painful feeling arises, simply name the feeling, like this: "That's anger. Anger. Anger. Oh, there's fear. Fear. Fear. Noticing disappointment. Disappointment. Disappointment."

4. After you've named your troubling emotions, continue to breathe mindfully and add a simple "yes" to the end of each name. For example, say quietly to yourself, *Anger—yes, fear—yes, disappointment—yes,* and so on.

5. You may start to feel a strong desire to change or fix something or to push it away. The urge to avoid painful emotions in this moment is a common response. That is why welcoming each upsetting feeling and saying yes to it helps you to move past any resistance and opens the opportunity for feelings to be cradled in the gentle, thoughtful arms of mindfulness.

What do you notice about the thoughts or beliefs that may perpetuate your anger, or that feed your resistance to your upset, fear, disappointment, and so on? You may begin to notice how resisting difficult emotions only perpetuates your suffering and pain. By staying present with your anger and other difficult emotions, and dropping your urge to avoid or resist them, you may find yourself struggling less and less, feeling lighter and lighter, calmer and calmer.

9.

Living Out Your Values Through Work

Jon Kabat-Zinn, the father of mindfulness-based stress reduction, at times asks people, "What is your job with a capital *J*?" (1994, 206)

One way of understanding this question is that Kabat-Zinn is pointing to us the possibility that how we invest our life energy in each action, or each relationship, or each moment can be a direct reflection of what we hold most sacred and true in our own lives.

Another person might phrase it differently, for example, "What is the reason I am here in this life?" or "What is my heart calling me to do in this world?"

The really interesting—and inspiring—thing is that we all must find the answer for ourselves. We must also trust that we will know it is our "job with a capital *J*" because, if we pay close enough attention, we will feel—all the way to our bones—the joy of embodying our deepest values in actions and words in the changing conditions of each moment!

Perhaps you are in that "job with a capital *J*" now, and the challenge for you is to sustain interest and attention in the face of very real challenges to success and demands on your time and energy. Or perhaps you are seeking a different job, and have come to view your present job as not so important or not worth your efforts. In this case, do you find yourself disengaging from work, lacking focus, or perhaps even becoming irritated or resentful?

Or perhaps you have never really inquired about your deepest values at all, or what gives you meaning and purpose. Maybe you have not actually considered that any job could serve you that way.

Try this meditation to reflect upon and explore your values and work experience mindfully, and learn more about your "job with a capital *J*."

1. Prepare for this mindful reflection and practice by taking some time for yourself, choosing a time when you will not be interrupted. Place some paper and a pen (or your computer) nearby, and sit quietly.

2. Begin by spending some time in meditation, practicing any of the core meditations from chapter 2 for several minutes, or longer if you like. If you don't know where to start, mindful breathing is always a good choice.

3. When you are ready, make a list of the qualities that are most important to you and which you would most like to share in your work and in the world. It can be a short list or a longer list. You might list qualities such as *kind, brave, generous, loving, loyal, reliable, well-liked*, or *effective*, for example. As you are making your list, pause and breathe mindfully from time to time.

4. When you feel finished, stop writing and breathe mindfully for a few breaths.

5. Bring attention back to your list, and choose one to three of the values that are most important to you.

6. Spend time over the next few days, in meditation and in daily life, reflecting on your top three values and looking for ways you might nurture or express those values in your job now.

7. If you don't think you can express those values in your current job, spend time mindfully reflecting on what prevents that. Could that change? Could you change in such a way that you can more strongly express each value in your daily actions and words?

CHAPTER 6

Beyond Your Angry Mind: Practices for Living with More Joy and Peace in Every Moment

A group of people come together for an afternoon of intensive mindfulness meditation practice. After three hours of silent practice, they share their experiences with each other.

A middle-aged man reports that he realized how much of his always keeping busy is an effort to hide a deeper pain inside, and how he has resolved to slow down and heal that pain. A woman in her midthirties has noticed that her grief for a dying relative is now balanced by a new appreciation for the beauty of nature, which that relative enjoyed and with which she connected during her meditations. A man in his late sixties reflects that he now feels more freedom from his inner judges and his usual sense of restless urgency. He can now relax more and allow things to happen in their own time.

In mindfulness-based stress reduction (MBSR) classes, one of the basic beliefs is that, no matter how much people believe is wrong with them, there is more right than is wrong. You do not have to actually be in an MBSR class for this to be true! Much of what is "more right" about people is their ability to be mindful, to touch their enormous reserve of kindness and compassion, and to discover the strength and wisdom within that can help them remain present for, and transform, any pain or distress they may be carrying in themselves or that they may face in others. Practicing with any of the meditations in this book can help you touch your own mindfulness, kindness, and capacity for understanding, and discover what is "more right than is wrong" for yourself!

From the perspective of mindfulness practice, life always happens in the present moment. When feelings of anger, hostility, despair, or criticism and judgment storm over you, they are only temporary conditions. They do not define you; nor do they represent all you can be as a human being.

The mindfulness-based meditations throughout this book point repeatedly—in a variety of situations and relationships—to the possibility for new and positive experiences within the unfolding conditions of daily life, even when the first reaction in any of those moments is anger or ill will. Any situation you find yourself in, and any emotion you feel, will change anyway. How you turn attention to what is present and happening—or don't—makes all the difference. If you want a happier, more peaceful, less angry life, you can find it. You do not have to wait for others to change or for a better world magically to appear. You can change yourself with mindfulness, compassion, and wisdom, and discover new possibilities and wonders available to you right here, right now. You can find out for yourself that the extraordinary is already here, simply waiting for you to notice it in the familiar routines of living every day.

In this book, we have been exploring—in narrative and directly through meditation practice—three fundamental meditative paths to managing and transforming anger. Those three paths are stopping and disentangling from the momentum of angry feelings in mind and body, turning to kindness and compassion when the storms of anger and aversion appear, and nurturing wise understanding about the basic causes and conditions that support anger so they can be altered or removed in any situation.

This chapter invites you to expand and deepen the focus of your experience with mindfulness even more. The practices you will find here are intended to—anytime you choose—help you remember, reconnect, and live from a place that is calmer and more aware, sensitive, appreciative, and life-affirming.

The practices here are closely related to the seven core mindfulness-based meditations you learned in chapter 2, in the sense that they are not motivated by nor do they necessarily begin with angry feelings. With those core meditations and these practices as well, you definitely don't have to wait until you are angry to practice mindfulness, compassion, or wisdom! These practices point to a world that is here and waiting for your attention in each moment—a world that constantly arises and changes as life touches and interacts with your whole being.

Experiencing for yourself, even for a single mindful breath, that you actually do possess the capacity for greater awareness, presence, and positive qualities such as generosity, humor, awe, compassion, and other expressions of basic human goodness, is possible. These practices encourage you to return—in many different ways, on purpose, and more often—to the place in you that is more right than wrong. They hold the promise of helping to ground you in an always-present peaceful, enduring center, and they offer the opportunity for you to open yourself up in deeper and more satisfying ways to the beauty and mystery that is always here and now, waiting for you.

On the pages that follow, you will find nine mindfulness practices to help you again experience directly the depths of peace, beauty, and mystery that are possible in your life.

How to Respond Mindfully
to the Pain of Others

A man waits in pre-op for his minor surgery procedure. He is calm and eagerly anticipates the procedure, which will restore a vital bodily function. As he waits, he notices the day-surgery staff members around him are becoming increasingly agitated, and one person in particular seems especially distracted and distressed. He notices his thoughts begin to go toward concern for himself, wondering if they might be too stressed to do a good job on his procedure. Because he has had mindfulness training, he recognizes this fear in himself and decides to do something else with the feelings of agitation and stress that seem to fill this room and that are creeping into his own mind. He begins to breathe mindfully, gathering attention on his own breath and stepping back out of his imagined fears. After a few moments, he shifts his attention, and imagines that with each in-breath he is actually inhaling the stress and pain around him as if it were smoke that was filling the room. He takes the "smoke" in fully, imagining that it fills his heart, where it is cleaned and purified; and on the out-breath, he releases the breath and imagines it as a cool breeze of peace, ease, and clarity that flows into the room and surrounds everyone there. After a few minutes pass, he notices that he has become calmer and, for whatever the reason, so have most of the others.

It might seem strange to think that turning toward and deliberately taking on the pain of another could lead to profound peace and ease and change in ourselves, but looking deeper, we may realize it is not so strange, possibly because it reminds us to return to the place in us that is still, aware, and compassionate, and that senses the truth of interconnection and belonging.

The conditions of life, which are interdependent, constantly change and flow through the present moment. If we are present and pay attention, we cannot fail to notice that pain in ourselves as well as in others is often a condition we observe in this moment. And with mindfulness, there is always something we can do to help.

1. In a situation where you notice the pain of others and there is nothing more your actions or words seem to be able to change, breathe mindfully for at least a minute, longer if you like.

2. Set an intention for your practice. Perhaps it could be, "May this practice bring ease and peace to everyone here."

3. Shift attention to the pain and stress that you sense, and with each in-breath, imagine you are taking the stress into your heart, like oily smoke, until you feel your body filled with the breath. As

you are breathing in, you can whisper silently to yourself, *Breathing in, I take in the pain of these others, so that it can be transformed.* Trusting that the goodness and wisdom within you is vast and powerful enough to transform this pain, steady your attention on your breathing, and let the transformation happen.

4. On your out-breath, imagine you are breathing out a cool breeze of peace, ease, and calm. If you like, you can whisper silently to yourself, *Breathing out, I release the cool breeze of peace, ease, and calm.* Following the sensations of the out-breath to the very end, allow yourself to rest in the stillness that follows, before the next in-breath. Keep breathing mindfully, inhaling the stress and exhaling peace and ease, practicing this meditation as long as you like.

A word of caution: This can be a very challenging practice. Strong and upsetting feelings and thoughts can arise in you. But if you keep breathing mindfully, offering yourself compassion, and recognizing the changing and interdependent nature of thoughts and bodily reactions, you could be surprised at what you learn and feel! Practice and see what you might discover.

Finding Joy and Contentment

Is it possible to locate pockets of joy and contentment in the throes of anger and upset? You may feel it's counterintuitive that such opposing emotions can coexist. But what if we told you that mindfulness meditation offers the skills to access a broader spectrum of feelings beyond the confines of anger? This next technique may not provide instantaneous happiness. However, with practice, you will begin to experience the impermanence of anger, which will allow other emotions, such as joy and contentment, to come to the surface more readily. Mindfulness is an effective ally for discovering your joy and happiness again.

The following self-inquiry practice will aid you in being mindful of your angry thoughts and feelings in order to allow your joy and contentment to emerge.

1. Take this moment to pause and then drop into your breath mindfully, observing closely every detail of each in-breath and each out-breath. Remember, each breath is a bridge to the present moment. Connect with each breath now, following the sensation and flow of oxygen drawn in by your body and oxygen forced out by your body, without trying to change or alter your breathing

in any way. Simply let your breathing be what it is. Do this for several breaths.

2. Next, set your intention for this practice, or what you hope to gain by it. On your next in-breath, say aloud or to yourself, *May this practice help me to accept my feelings with greater joy and contentment. May this practice connect me to the fullness of each emotion and each moment in life.*

3. If you feel a storm of anger arising, simply allow and acknowledge what is occurring. You may not know what caused your anger or why you feel outraged, but you can recognize and acknowledge the physical symptoms. You might notice your heart surges, your face feels hot and flushed, or your body shakes with fury. This is what anger feels like sometimes. Just be with the anger and let it be, without acting on it or trying to escape it.

4. Explore more deeply, with clarity and detachment, the facts about your experience of these angry emotions and thoughts. Notice how thoughts, feelings, and sensations are constantly changing. One moment the rage is forceful. The next moment the rage is replaced by minor annoyance. The next moment the annoyance is replaced by boredom. The next moment the boredom is replaced by anger again. Thoughts and emotions

cycle in and cycle out, and then recycle again. Just notice how no one thought or feeling stays the same. There is a continual and random shifting of thoughts, feelings, and sensations—coming and going, intensifying and then fading way.

5. Remind yourself to check in with your breath and be mindful of it.

6. Now, take this moment to bring to mind a time where you felt true inner joy and contentment. Maybe it was on your wedding night. Maybe it was the smile on your child's face this morning. Maybe it's a favorite photo of your best friend. What does that joy feel like for you? Where does that joy live in your mind and your body? Your joy might bring a smile to your face just thinking about it. Your joy may give you a warm, fuzzy feeling inside. Simply notice how joy bubbles up inside and out.

Remember, you carry this joy and contentment with you at all times. They are there to tap in to whenever you need them.

Becoming One with All That Is

Because of cultural, linguistic, and societal constructions of reality, most people are locked into thinking that they are separate and apart from others. When you feel angry thoughts and feelings, it's quite normal to feel isolated and abandoned because of your suffering and pain. You may experience bouts of loneliness, feeling withdrawn and misunderstood by others. Sometimes the pain is so great that you can't imagine anyone who could understand or feel your pain.

For this next practice, let's try an experiment by mindfully and consciously shifting your cultural awareness from "I" to "we" thinking. When you intentionally make yourself aware that you are connected to everyone and everyone is connected to you, you begin to notice that your pain is everyone's pain and everyone's pain is your pain. In this acknowledgement and awareness of how we are all one in our experience of suffering, you will begin the magical process of feeling interconnected with all others. You are no longer alone in your suffering.

1. Give yourself permission to stop whatever you're doing and be here for this practice.

2. Put gentle attention on the natural and auto-matic process of your breathing. It is really quite

extraordinary when you ponder it. The body knows how and when to breathe, involuntarily and miraculously. On your next in-breath, notice where the body takes in air most easily. On your next out-breath, notice where the body most easily releases the air. Focus on a place in your body where it most easily experiences the sensation of each breath, such as the tip of your nose, or your chest, or your belly. Do this for several breaths.

3. Now, take this moment to acknowledge that, as you breathe, the whole wide world is breathing with you. All living beings are breathing together, in unison. You are connected with all beings by this breath of life. You share the air, so you share each breath. No one breathes alone. You breathe, and the world breathes with you. We breathe as one. This is oneness.

4. When you feel ready, begin to pay purposeful attention to the thoughts, feelings, and sensations that come to mind for you at this time. What thoughts circulate in your mind? What emotions do you carry in your heart? What sensations do you notice in your body? If you are experiencing anger and loneliness, simply notice those feelings without putting judgment or blame on them. Let the feelings just be. If you notice disconnection from friends and family, simply be aware of

those thoughts without finding fault or getting caught up in the story behind the thoughts. Let the thoughts just be.

5. Now, take this unique moment in time to acknowledge that someone else, maybe close by or maybe very far away, is feeling angry, lonely, and abandoned. Consider the possibility that someone, somewhere, perhaps right now or at some other time, also struggles with feeling exactly what you're feeling. Just like you, there are others who are burdened with painful thoughts, emotions, and sensations. You are connected to others through your suffering. It is what everyone shares in common at all times. You are never truly alone.

Remember this wisdom of oneness throughout your day. Send loving-kindness and compassion to yourself and all beings on their journey.

4.

Growing in Gratitude

A wise mind is open to seeking a higher truth, such as gratitude, within anger. The next practice invites you to deepen your understanding of anger by connecting to the present moment and then exploring what you are grateful for, even when anger is present.

1. Begin by finding a place—where you won't be disturbed, if possible—to sit comfortably.

2. Mindfully connect with your breath. Follow each in-breath and out-breath and the space between them. Follow each breath, in and out, to the point where the breath ends.

3. Now, while you're paying attention to your breath and allowing each breath to naturally come to you, consider what thoughts and feelings are resting in your mind. If you're angry, notice the angry thoughts and feelings as if they were clouds moving across the sky. As thoughts and feelings come to mind, simply acknowledge them.

4. Continue to pay purposeful attention to your inner monologue of thoughts and feelings and

then gently note or name them without judgment, blame, or shame. For example, "I'm having an angry thought now—that's all it is. There's another angry feeling—that's all it is. I'm having mundane thoughts about chores—that's all they are. I'm having a sad feeling—that's all it is." Breathing mindfully, continue to name your thoughts and feelings in this nonjudgmental fashion. There's nothing that you need to do or change or work on. Let your thoughts simply pass on through like clouds moving across the sky, one after the other.

5. Return your focus to your breath. As you breathe in, consider all the wondrous bodily mechanisms that keep you alive within each breath. Your wise body knows exactly what to do to breathe and keep your heart beating, to breathe and keep your blood pumping, to breathe and keep your lungs functioning. The act of breathing is a perfectly choreographed dance of body parts and synchronized movement that gives you life. Pause mindfully to give gratitude for this life-sustaining process. On your in-breath, say to yourself, *Thank you for this body that breathes life into me.* On your out-breath, say to yourself, *Thank you for this breath of life.* Speak your gratitude for at least five to ten breaths.

As thoughts and feelings come and go, your body conducts the complicated task of breathing to keep you alive. Be grateful for your body. Make opportunities to express gratitude for this life. A wise mind understands that even as painful thoughts and feelings pass in and out of view, each breath holds a moment to acknowledge, with gratitude, the astounding workings of your body to support life. How does it feel to sit with your gratitude? Through gratitude, you will experience the wisdom of truth in your life—a wisdom that reaches beyond your anger.

5.

Moving Through Anger to Sacredness

Anger narrows your focus and makes it difficult to see the bigger picture. If you want to cultivate a life beyond your immediate experience of anger and upset, you'll want to find ways to break out of and free yourself from the destructive mind trap of anger. Let's try a mindfulness practice for moving through anger in order to get to the sacredness of life. Mindfulness will help you to get there by employing a few of your senses—sight, hearing, and touch. These will help you to connect more fully with the sacred beauty found all around you.

1. If you can be outside in nature, that would be ideal for this practice. If you can't be in nature, bring to mind a place of outdoor beauty and splendor. It might be a favorite spot along a river, a hiking trail, a beautiful beach, or a view of a mountain. Think about what you love most about this special place. It could be the crisp, fresh air, or the quiet stillness, or the sound of crashing ocean waves.

2. Bring purposeful awareness to your breath in your belly or abdomen. Follow the natural progression

of each in-breath and each out-breath, as the air flows in and out, your chest rising and falling.

3. Using your sense of sight, what do you notice and see around you? Pay close attention to every detail that catches your eye. Notice colors, shapes, textures, and dimensions. Notice the multitude of shades of green. Notice the leaves still on the tree branches and the ones on the ground. Notice the skyline and the way the angle of sun casts unusual shadows around you. Notice what is up close and what is far away. What catches your attention visually? Remember to simply breathe and watch mindfully.

4. Using your sense of hearing, what do you notice and hear around you? Pay close attention to every sound that enters your ears. You may hear children playing and giggling. You may hear the rush of a river. You may hear different birds chirping, some nearby, some further away. Notice how some sounds are piercing and strong, while others are subtle and nuanced. Notice how sounds come and go. What catches your ears? Remember to breathe and listen mindfully.

5. Leave behind the sounds and shift your focus on your sense of touch. What can you feel around

you? Pay close attention to everything that touches you physically. You may feel your clothes against your body and the fabric closest to your skin. You may feel the wind brushing your face or whipping through your hair. You may feel the warmth under your arms or your tongue resting in your mouth. Notice how what you feel changes and shifts. Remember to breathe mindfully and notice the physical sensation of touch.

6. Now, reflect on what is stirring emotionally in your heart. What came up for you while you were noticing the world around you using your senses of sight, hearing, and touch? You may feel more calm, connected, and grounded. Feel in this moment the sensation being surrounded by the beauty and sacredness of this place. This special place brims with life and wonder, and you experience it with awe—every grain of sand, every bird overhead, every fish in the sea, every drop of water. Each aspect is precious, rare, and extraordinary in its singular beauty. Breathe in this sacredness and let it fill your body with its exquisiteness. Allow yourself to be bathed in the light of splendor and awe, as you explore what is sacred to you.

6.

Finding Joy in the Good Fortune of Others

As our attention to ourselves and to the world around us grows more sensitive, more accurate, and more inclusive through mindfulness-based practice, we may begin to feel less contracted and appreciate more deeply the joy of others. Learning to recognize that joy and to support it rather than falling back into feelings of envy or self-centeredness (which are often conducive to anger) can promote a powerful opening of our heart and human spirit: we recognize that ordinary people, like us, can experience joy in ordinary things.

For example, when your neighbors tell you they are headed off on a dream vacation, what is your first reaction? For many, it could be self-centered, something like, "I wish I could take a vacation like that." That is okay; it is only natural to respond that way. But instead of going to the place of envy and diminished self-worth, what if instead you cultivated taking joy in the joy of others?

A simple meditative practice called "sympathetic joy" can help you cultivate responding to the good fortune of others by taking joy in their joy. In the example of the neighbors and the vacation, even though you may notice your ego-mind wishing for its own vacation, you might also, noticing mindfully, sense the joy in your neighbors, and turn to share and support it. Feeling the joy in them and in the moment, you might speak deeply from your heart of generosity, saying something like, "Have a great trip! May your good fortune and happiness never end."

The practice of sympathetic joy can be a formal meditation, or it can be a part of a spontaneous moment, just as when the neighbors tell us about their vacation. Sympathetic joy uses phrases as a focus and is a close relative of the core meditations of loving-kindness and compassion that we explored in chapter 2. Whereas those practices utilize phrases based in kindness and compassion for self and others, this practice focuses on sensing and supporting the joy in another person. Doing that can lead to the interesting discovery that our joy is deeply interwoven with the joy of others. Here are some phrases you might experiment with in responding to another person or bringing that person into your heart during a period of formal meditation: "May your good fortune never end," "May you always have such happiness in your life," "May this happiness never leave you," "May your peace and joy continue."

Can you think of other phrases to express sympathetic joy?

7.

How to Offer Benevolence and Goodwill

If you hang around with your anger long enough, you'll act cranky and rude to others. You might find yourself speaking unkindly to someone you care about. You might be curt and impatient with a coworker. You might be unfriendly or disrespectful with a salesclerk or a stranger. Later, you might feel guilt and regret about what you said or how you treated that person. It may be too late to apologize in person, but it's never too late to offer goodwill and benevolence to others in spirit.

1. Start by sitting quietly and settling into a comfortable and safe space. Check in with your posture and make sure you are alert and attentive.

2. Bring your awareness to your breath, following each breath as it comes and goes naturally, in and out of your body.

3. Set your intentions for this practice, such as "May this practice help me to be aware of when my anger affects other people," "May this practice remind me to act and speak with goodness in my

heart," or "May this practice restore goodwill and kindheartedness to others."

4. Now, bring to mind someone that you might have had an unpleasant exchange with, however brief. Without ruminating on the entire uncomfortable conversation or berating yourself for any single unkind or grouchy remark that you might have made, simply hold an image of this person in your mind's eye.

5. On your next breath, visualize wholeheartedly bestowing goodwill and benevolence to this person who was on the receiving end of your anger. With each breath, imagine this person's heart filling with the light of loving-kindness and tenderness. Imagine this person feeling acknowledged and appreciated. There is no need to blame or feel shame. There is just awareness, acknowledgment, and appreciation to be offered. How does it feel to extend this goodwill?

6. Feel free to bring to mind other people who might have brushed shoulders with your angry tone or comment. Take this time to visualize each person's heart bathed in the light of goodwill and kindness. They feel your offer of loving-kindness and tenderness from afar. They feel wholeheartedly and sincerely acknowledged and appreciated

by you. Again, check in with your heart and explore what comes up for you when you extend goodwill.

During times of distressful conversations or when unkind words are exchanged, remember to wish goodness and kindness to yourself and others. It may not come easy at first and it may not replace a sincere apology, but with practice, it will help you find new ways to react when you're angry. In time, it will help reduce negative interactions and circulate more generosity and benevolence to yourself and others.

8.

How to Rebuild Your Self-Worth

Anger issues can wreak havoc on your sense of self-worth. After an angry episode, you may beat yourself up, berate yourself, or damn yourself for not handling the situation differently or more calmly. After an angry outburst, you may unleash your mean self-critic, undermining your self-esteem and self-dignity. You may say negative things to yourself, such as *I hate myself when my anger takes over, I'm unworthy of love when I act out in anger,* or *I don't deserve good things in life when I rage inside and out.*

Your anger doesn't make you a bad person. Your anger is just a reaction, separate from who you really are and all the characteristics that make this up. The following mindfulness practice will help free you from negative self-criticism in order to rebuild your sense of self-worth and self-regard. Try it now.

1. First, congratulate yourself for making time for this meditation. This is an important step in moving closer to your self-healing and well-being. Praise yourself with kindness for taking this time.

2. Take a comfortable position in a place where you will not be distracted or interrupted.

3. Gently tune your awareness in on your breath, letting air move in and air move out of your body.

4. Allow your awareness to become increasingly caring and nurturing.

5. Give yourself permission to just be here. You don't need to go anywhere, or be anywhere, or call anyone, or engage with anything. You're free to do nothing except be here now.

6. When negative self-talk comes to mind, simply notice it and listen with tenderness and sensitivity, as if you were listening to a small child. The child might say, "I'm bad. I hate myself. I hurt other people." Whatever harsh words come up, imagine tossing them into a river and watching them drift downstream, being carried away.

7. Continue to breathe mindfully with soft attention and gentle awareness.

8. Return to the river and notice the negative thoughts and feelings floating on the river, moving with the current. What do you notice as you continue to sprinkle your harsh criticisms into the river? Notice the ebb and flow of these critical thoughts and feelings. Notice how they flood in and then dissipate. Notice how they start to

change and are replaced by different thoughts and feelings. Some of these new thoughts might be mean-spirited. Some might be trivial or mundane. Some might be silly or frivolous. Simply notice how your thoughts and feelings are always evolving, coming and then going, magnifying and then receding.

9. Feel supported and held with each mindful breath.

Meet any thought with empathy and softheartedness. Meet any emotion with kindness and sensitivity. Offer your thoughts and emotions clemency and compassion.

9.

Transforming Anger with Compassion

Most people who struggle with anger form a habitual response or reaction to their anger, particularly anger directed toward others. They feel immense pain, sadness, remorse, and helplessness after directing their anger toward someone. Your anger may cause you to feel defeated, vulnerable, and helpless to change it. You may wish you could leave town or take it all back. You may also experience an intense urge to vent, lash out, break something, or be self-destructive. Over time, this reaction can feel like a permanent or unalterable response. But it doesn't have to be. What if you could train yourself to respond to angry thoughts and feelings by providing loving-kindness and compassion to yourself and others?

You may find it unimaginable that you could respond to anger with wholehearted tenderness and understanding, but it's possible—with practice of course. The following mindfulness and compassion practice will strengthen your ability to respond to anger with kindness and empathy.

1. You can do this meditation anywhere—sitting, standing, or lying down—as long as you keep alert and awake.

2. Bring your awareness to your breath, and breathe mindfully. If you like, narrow your focus to the

sound of your breathing and listen. Notice the sound of air rushing in and air rushing out. Listen intently for a minute or two.

3. When you feel more settled in and relaxed, shift your awareness to a painful or distressing situation. What thoughts and feelings do you have? Notice any thoughts or feelings of being bitter, fearful, overwhelmed, or regretful for how the situation unfolded. Simply take note and let it be.

4. As you continue to focus on yourself, speak directly to your heart where your pain and suffering are most present. Speak softly with tenderness and compassion, as if you were bestowing a sacred blessing over a sick friend. You can use these phrases or make up your own: "May I live in joy and contentment," "May I live free from harm," "May I live in peace and ease of mind and body," "May I live with good health and well-being."

5. Now, shift your focus to someone with whom you're feeling angry—or someone who might have been the recipient of your anger. When you have a person in mind, speak directly to the heart of that person who may be experiencing pain and suffering in his or her life at this moment. Remember to speak gently and tenderly with empathy and compassion. You can use these phrases or make up your own: "May you live in joy and contentment,"

"May you live free from harm," "May you live in peace and ease of mind and body," "May you live with good health and well-being."

6. Return to your breath. Within each in-breath and out-breath is a mindful opportunity to reconnect with the present moment.

7. Now, broaden your focus and imagine all the people around the globe who may be experiencing pain and suffering in their hearts at this time. Speak to them warmly and sensitively, with understanding and compassion. You can use these phrases or make up your own: "May all people live in joy and contentment," "May all people live free from harm," "May all people live in peace and ease of mind and body," "May all people live with good health and well-being."

Remember to embrace your upsetting thoughts and feelings with kindness and without judgment. When anger arises, get in the practice of extending love and compassion to your heart and to the hearts of others.

Epilogue

We live in the present moment.

Our inner life of thoughts, emotions, bodily sensations, and other sense experiences; the complex outer world of others; and life unfolding around us—all these things meet in the here and now. These worlds, inner and outer, are constantly changing and interacting.

In any moment, how aware are you of this changing flow and exchange between the inner and outer worlds—between yourself and others? How much of the inner life are you aware of? How steady is your attention to the flow in both worlds? Is your heart filled with welcome and curiosity for what is here—inside or outside—or have dullness of mind, fear, dislike, rejection, or anger created a sense of being cut off and alone?

Maybe you think you should be a certain way, or that the world should be different. Our tendency is to try to become something, so we set an ideal, some goal, for how we should be different. But, in this moment, things are as they are, and *we* are as we are. We must begin here, with knowing how things are now instead of becoming lost in how we or anything else "should be."

Mindfulness is available to each of us in any moment. It is the good "mirror," you might say, that can both accurately reflect what is happening in our inner world and illuminate the world that is manifesting around us—just as it is, right now.

Practicing mindfulness is a process of awakening. Using the mirror of mindfulness to reflect what is present in and around us, we bring awareness through sensitive attention to the conditions of mind and body that are here now—sensations of pain or pleasure, or memories, or thoughts and opinions. These conditions are ordinary ones in the sense that they are so common, and don't depend upon special circumstances. We can also notice the equally ordinary sensations of breathing or walking with the same watchful attention. They are here, now. We let them be, and we watch them carefully and kindly. And by bringing awareness to all these things, we begin to see them differently. They can be seen as objects rather than as an identity, as "me" or "mine." This shift in perspective means we can begin to find some space, perhaps enter a dimension of awareness always available, that presents many more choices. It can be this way, too—more awareness, more space, and more choice—with any feelings of anger and ill will we have as well as any impulses to condemn, criticize, or reject anyone or anything sharing this moment with us.

This work of mindfulness and meditation practice can also be challenging. It is a very special kind of work, an inner work that is based in growing sensitivity to and awareness of the true nature of your thoughts, feelings, and other experiences as an embodied human being. It can lead to radical shifts in your perspective, to the questioning of assumptions and ideas you have held about what it means to be "you."

Doing the work of mindfulness and meditation, we can see more clearly how to live in this world as well as with ourselves and others, as we learn how to work with strong emotions like anger and with the thoughts and fears that fuel them. On the level of daily life, mindfulness helps us see what brings harmony and ease, and what does not. Seeing more mindfully, we can reliably touch our deepest values, observe more of our own process of awakening, and see more clearly our role in relationships and in the world. What is our function? How can we contribute? What can we contribute? The meaning of our lives lies in what we choose and make our lives to be. Practicing mindfulness can help you find that meaning. What will you choose?

We close this book with these wishes for you:

May mindfulness in its most universal expression flower in your life, and may you discover the boundlessness, courage, and dignity of your human heart.

May you find the peaceful, enduring center within and learn to dwell there with unshakable joy, ease, and wisdom in any circumstance.

May you experience your capacity for exceptional presence, compassion, and kindness, and share that with others.

When you offer your voice and actions to the world, may you offer to others the gifts of safety and well-being, and may countless others benefit from your being who you most deeply are.

References

Davidson, R. J., with S. Begley. 2012. *The Emotional Life Of Your Brain: How Its Unique Patterns Affect the Way You Think, Feel, and Live—and How You Can Change Them.* New York: Hudson Street Press.

Feldman, C. 2001. *The Buddhist Path to Simplicity: Spiritual Practice for Everyday Life.* London: Thorsons.

Fredrickson, B. 2009. *Positivity: Groundbreaking Research Reveals How to Embrace the Hidden Strength of Positive Emotions, Overcome Negativity, and Thrive.* New York: Crown Publishers.

Goleman, D. 1997. *Emotional Intelligence: Why It Can Matter More Than IQ.* New York: Bantam Books.

———. 2003. *Destructive Emotions: How Can We Overcome Them? A Scientific Dialogue with the Dalai Lama.* New York: Bantam Books.

Kabat-Zinn, J. 1994. *Wherever You Go There You Are: Mindfulness Meditation in Everyday Life.* New York: Hyperion.

———. 2013. *Full Catastrophe Living: Using the Wisdom of Your Body and Mind to Face Stress, Pain, and Illness.* Revised and updated edition. New York: Bantam Books.

Salzberg, S. 2008. *The Kindness Handbook: A Practical Companion.* Boulder, CO: Sounds True.

Williams, M., J. Teasdale, Z. Segal, and J. Kabat-Zinn. 2007. *The Mindful Way Through Depression: Freeing Yourself from Chronic Unhappiness.* New York: Guilford Press.

Jeffrey Brantley, MD, is a consulting associate in the department of psychiatry and Behavioral Sciences at Duke University, and the founder and director of the Mindfulness-Based Stress Reduction Program at Duke Integrative Medicine. He has done multiple radio, television, and print media interviews regarding the MBSR program at Duke. He is author of *Calming Your Anxious Mind* and coauthor of *Daily Meditations for Calming Your Anxious Min d*, *Five Good Minutes*, *Five Good Minutes in the Evening*, *Five Good Minutes at Work*, *Five Good Minutes with the One You Love*, and *Five Good Minutes in Your Body*.

Wendy Millstine, NC, is a freelance writer and certified holistic nutrition consultant who specializes in diet and stress reduction. With Jeffrey Brantley, she is coauthor of the *Five Good Minutes*® series, *Daily Meditations for Calming Your Anxious Mind*, and *True Belonging*. Millstine is also coauthor of *Calming the Rush of Panic*. She lives in Santa Rosa, CA.

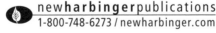